WHAT TO DO WHEN THE PEOPLE YOU WORK WITH DRIVE YOU CRAZY

Lynne Eisaguirre

BUSINESS

AVON, MASSACHUSETTS

Published by Adams Business
An imprint of Adams Media, an F+W Publications Company
57 Littlefield Street
Avon, MA 02322
www.adamsmedia.com

ISBN-10: 1-59337-548-4
ISBN-13: 978-1-59337-548-5

Library of Congress Cataloging-in-Publication Data
is available from the publisher.

Printed in the United States of America.

J I H G F E D C B A

The author acknowledges kind permission to reprint material appearing on
pages 46–48, reprinted from *Social Intelligence: The New Science of Human
Relationships* by Daniel Goleman, Copyright © 2006 by Daniel Goleman.
Used by permission of Bantam Books, a division of Random House, Inc.;
and on page 196, reprinted from *In Control* by Redford Williams, MD, and
Virginia Williams, PhD. Copyright © 2006 by Redford Williams, MD, and
Virginia Williams, PhD. Permission granted by Rodale, Inc.

*This book is available at quantity discounts for bulk purchases.
For information, please call 1-800-289-0963.*

CONTENTS

ACKNOWLEDGMENTS

Books are written by authors, but actually delivering a copy into a reader's hands takes much more than one person's work. I'm indebted to my agent, Michael Snell, who came to me with the proposal for this book. Jill Alexander at Adams Media created the original concept, and helped me shape and refocus the content, while remaining cheerful and optimistic—everything a writer wants an editor to be. Meredith O'Hayre added her expert editorial eye to the final manuscript.

My hard-working and upbeat assistant, Shannon Duran, typed and proofed endless versions of this book without complaint. O. C. O'Connell offered last-minute editing and research. I'm thankful to many clients who trusted me with their personal stories. Their names and identities have been changed in many situations to protect the innocent.

Friends Bill Cahal, Peter Clarke, Susan Hazaleus, and Val Moses helped shore up my attitude. My fellow "villagers," residents of my co-housing community in Golden, Colorado, offered in-the-trenches training on the realities of dealing with different personalities, thorny conflicts, and the consensus process.

I'm grateful to neuropsychologist Dr. Debra Holden and psychiatrist Dr. Ron Rabin for patiently explaining brain function. Any mistakes in this area, however, are my own.

My parents, Joe and Wilma Eisaguirre, and siblings, Kim Jones and Lew Eisaguirre, provided moral support and their usual unflagging belief in my abilities—as well as teaching me much of what I know about difficult people! (That's a joke, guys!)

On the home front, Allison King helped care for my children with devoted attention so that I would have the time and energy to work. John Evans provided moral support as well as extra child care. And of course my kids, Elizabeth and Nicholas, worked cheerfully on their own books so that I would have the time to write mine. I love you more than any writer's words can ever express.

Introduction
HOW TO MOVE FROM PISSED OFF
TO POWERFUL

Hint: Accept that difficult people work everywhere.

Even on a good day, you can name at least one difficult person at the office. On a bad day you can probably rattle off four or five without even pausing. Be they slackers, sneaks, liars, tyrants, boors, bullies, wimps, whiners, workaholics, or everyday incompetents, you've got your hands full with people who are making it difficult for you to do your job well and stay sane.

I know this because my entire work life revolves around helping people deal with difficult people and workplace conflict. Nonetheless, I do love my work. I love making a difference in how organizations function, how people collaborate, and I get a charge out of how improving those skills improves workplace performance. It's a direct boost to the bottom line.

Understanding each other, one person at a time, finding common ground in everyday interactions, and negotiating differences is essential at every workplace in every corner of the globe. Why? Your personal happiness is at stake. Your company's future is at stake. Every department within your company needs to enhance performance. Collaboration, creative problem-solving, and negotiating conflict is the golden ticket.

Everybody wants to talk about creating high-performance teams, hardwiring organizational excellence, and improving emotional intelligence. However, all of these require the ability to deal with conflict. You must be able to negotiate with people who may not look or sound anything like you. You've got to be able to bridge differences. That's where *Stop Pissing Me Off!* comes in.

They're Everywhere

I regularly do keynote addresses, seminars, and consulting engagements on this subject. Invariably, after every program, people swarm the podium to confirm that our corporations are overflowing with difficult people. I listen to a litany of horror stories in which the storyteller is victimized by some difficult person. The puzzling part is that *no one* ever claims to be the difficult one. What's up with that? What's up is that people almost always find a way to shift accountability, to believe that *they* are being wronged by difficult coworkers. They believe that if only those difficult people would shape up, their work lives would be better. That's true. Too bad it doesn't work that way all the time.

TAKE CONTROL

The thing is, it doesn't matter if the rascals don't take the initiative to shape up. You can still change the way interactions with those difficult people play out. Regardless of whether we're talking about a bully or whiner, your fate is not determined by the whims of your colleagues. In fact, it's quite the opposite. It's a little-known truth that you can change the entire dynamic that exists between you and those difficult people who routinely annoy you. It's not rocket science, nor is there some quick cure-all. It is simply a matter of adding some rather ordinary, but effective tools to your relationship tool box. To help make this easier, you'll find a handy list of such tools at the end of every chapter.

Every workplace has difficult people; yours is no exception. Perhaps *you* are even the difficult person in your workplace. Either way—whether you're the difficult person or a saint—you can transform your workplace into a place where you actually enjoy working. If you're thinking, "Huh, she doesn't know how bad it is at my job," I beg to differ. I've been to thousands of offices, assembly lines, R & D labs, quality control departments, executive team meetings, employee town hall gatherings, boiler rooms, back offices, frontline service operations, support areas, management retreats, call centers, break rooms, and board meetings. You don't know the trouble I've seen. I've helped organizations in the middle of ugly mergers, during massive layoffs, and when multimillion-dollar projects have blown up. I've worked with organizations that have swallowed up and spit out their best people and churned through CEOs by the second. I've seen plenty of outrageous ugliness and helped many an employee, manager, and executive turn around seemingly impossible situations.

Don't be cynical—change can happen. In fact, change happens one person at a time. Negotiating differences is a one-on-one exercise requiring a skill set that many people don't have and haven't known how to obtain. This book will get you there. I have been teaching these tactics and techniques for more than twenty years. They work. You'll get results. There's no gimmick; it's about using commonsense, tried-and-true communication techniques. It's about skills. It's about strategies. These are learned behaviors. If you're still reading this, you've demonstrated your capacity to learn, so you can rest easy; you're going to succeed at this.

What You'll Learn in This Book

This book is your emergency survive and *thrive* guide. As Juliet B. Schor writes in *The Overworked American: The Unexpected Decline of Leisure*, most of us spend more time at work than we do with our families. About 25 percent of that time is spent negotiating with others. Despite that statistic, we actually spend very little time learning how to resolve disputes skillfully. This practical and hard-hitting book will help you:

- Understand why so many people get crabby at work
- Put the brakes on a bad day
- Learn how to have difficult and successful conversations with difficult people
- Manage bozo bosses, crusty colleagues, and cranky customers
- Realize the benefits of sending yourself to time-out
- Survive and thrive in any workplace

The Consequences of Not Resolving Difficulties

One of my client scenarios, for example, involved a guy named Michael Tucker who was on the fast track at an upstart technology company. He was chosen to participate in that company's Management Development Program, and that opportunity came with some big-ticket benefits—an impressive promotion, a hefty salary, stock options, and plenty of perks after he successfully completed the training.

Michael was a thoughtful, introspective person who pondered issues before responding to questions. He liked to plan and weigh options before taking action. He avoided conflict whenever possible, fleeing from the fray like a roadrunner. He took a low profile until the coast was clear. He was a good guy.

The problem is that Michael couldn't seem to work with Grace Oberman, the office manager. Grace was well known for her unorthodox but productive ways. In fact, Grace's nickname was "GO" because of her initials and efficiency. She thrived on action. She constantly asked Michael to "cut to the chase" and harassed him when she thought he was dawdling in making decisions. No hemming and hawing for her. Grace relished the back-and-forth of debates and she usually triumphed in most arguments through force and ferociousness. She was a classic pit bull; Michael's cautious, thoughtful process incensed her. Both Michael and Grace whined to their coworkers, spouses, and therapists that the other party was so "difficult" to work with. After eighteen months of stop and go, neither Michael nor Grace was with the company any more. Their inability to resolve their differences cost them their job satisfaction and cost the company two great employees. This happens every week in companies just like yours all over the country. Small businesses, multinational corporations, nonprofits, family-owned enterprises—they all have employees who suffer from an inability to negotiate differences.

DEALING WITH DIFFERENCES

The workforce is more diverse than at any time in history. Organizations are a patchwork of people whose backgrounds vary widely—it is no longer a bastion of Caucasian males with a similar view of the world. Baby boomers, Gen X'ers, women, senior citizens, African Americans, Latinos, Asians, gays, lesbians, single parents, and dual-income families are some of the people creating our eclectic work environment. The divide among some—whether it's age, education, gender, position, values, socioeconomic background, political beliefs, or religion—

is a stumbling block to a productive work relationship. These differences frequently lead people to label others as "difficult." Learning how to work with different coworkers is no longer optional. It's essential; you can't have functional work teams without knowing how to deal with a wide variety of people effectively. It's a basic skill set that's as vital as computer literacy. Moreover, diversity is a gift because it allows your department, work team, or company to look at business challenges from a multitude of perspectives, and that creates new solutions. According to the Bureau of Labor Statistics, unemployment has hovered around 4 percent for more than two years now, with little sign of change. Even with the recent layoffs, there still aren't nearly enough qualified workers available for the jobs that are open. In fact, organizations that have suffered recent layoffs, mergers, acquisitions, or other transitions face even more conflict, created by the stress of change and uncertainty.

The bottom line: Organizations can't afford to have their ranks riddled with dissatisfaction and tension. They will lose star performers to their competitors if they don't foster an environment that appropriately deals with difficult people and cultivates a culture of tolerance, creativity, and collaboration.

The Value of a Proactive Approach

It used to be that I often got called just *after* a company had lost someone due to conflict. I'd fly in after the fact and assess the damage and help sort out the whole mess. There is a big shift that's occurring now. These days, I often get called *before* there's irreversible damage. People are starting to see that they can be proactive. The good news is that you don't have to depend upon your boss or your budget to learn these skills. You've now got *Stop Pissing Me Off!*

This book is unlike anything currently on the shelves. Sure, there are books on relationship conflicts, but there is no business book that deals with workplace woes resulting from the difficult people that populate your corridors. This is the only book that singularly tackles the issue of embracing difficult people in the workplace and offers the possibility of transforming those relationships. The tools in this book can transform your work life faster than any other change you can make. Not bad return on investment (ROI) on a book that is only slightly more than the price of a few designer cups of coffee!

This is not an academic tome—it's a field guide for people in the trenches at all levels of business who need to understand the underlying reasons for difficult people, manage those difficulties, work productively with a diverse work force, and transform work misery into work joy!

Had Michael and Grace read this book, they'd probably be happily ensconced in their respective offices, loving their jobs.

Why You and Your Organization Need This Book

Research from the American Management Association (AMA) shows that the staggering cost of replacing an employee can range from 30 percent of the employee's annual salary to 1.5 times that much. Moreover, the AMA also reports that turnover in the United States shot to its highest level in nearly two decades, reaching a record 19 percent in 2006. To put that in context, suppose a financial services firm employs 1,000 people at an average pay rate of $14 per hour. If that company has only a 10 percent turnover rate, the annual impact on its profits conservatively ranges from $875,000 to a whopping $1.2 million.

Reducing turnover is a mandate for organizations that wish to be successful. The top reason that employees leave is conflict with bosses and colleagues. The Gallup Organization interviewed two million employees at 700 different companies and found that employees' relationships with their supervisors affect how long they stay at a company as well as employee productivity. Marcus Buckingham, a senior management consultant at Gallup and the primary analyst for the study says, "People join companies and leave managers."

These results are corroborated by another recent survey about workplace stress. A Wright Management survey this year found that two-thirds of workers feel burned out. The highest source of stress? Difficult coworkers. Likewise, in my experience as a workplace consultant, the biggest reason people give for leaving their job is because they are disconnected from their bosses or work situation. Good people simply won't continue to work for jerks or toil under unfavorable daily conditions.

An interview of *Fortune* 500 senior executives reveals a statistic that can cripple businesses: Executives spend a significant amount of time wrestling with the difficult people at work who create unproductive conflict. In fact, 20 percent of their time is devoted to conflict-related activities. Think about that time in terms of money: 20 percent of their salary is wasted on unproductive conflict. Where's the ROI there? When you add up the costs of conflicts with difficult people, it's readily apparent that it can close the doors of organizations. There are the direct costs, productivity costs, opportunity costs, and the emotional costs that cause people to misdirect their energy to their own detriment.

Employees, supervisors, managers, and top executives all can use *Stop Pissing Me Off!* to gain the understanding, attitude, and skills they need to reduce turnover, create exceptional teams, and improve productivity. This book is full of practical examples and proven methods that represent some of the best practices for a productive workplace.

The power of this book is that it illuminates a productive path through conflicts with difficult people. It teaches you how to improve your own skills and become more successful, regardless of how others act or what relationship styles they use. You'll be a better individual contributor or leader, and a more skilled negotiator capable of facilitating resolutions in a business environment that is fraught with continuous change.

Because of my experience in diverse workplaces, I can relate to many different kinds of people, from truck drivers to technology experts. I've toiled as an attorney and intern for the U.S. Congress and federal government, and in law firms as an associate, contract attorney, and partner. I grew up working on a ranch and worked my way through college and law school by teaching swimming, cleaning restrooms, waiting tables, and washing dishes. I also worked as a dorm counselor and secretary. Trust me: Difficult people populated all those diverse work situations, so I had at least thirty years of working experience to draw on while writing this book.

If you travel the yellow brick road of this book, I guarantee you'll have better work days ahead, and who knows? You might even get in to see the wizard.

YOUR RELATIONSHIP TOOLBOX

HOW TO MOVE FROM PISSED OFF TO POWERFUL

PISSED OFF	POWERFUL
Searching for a place without difficult people	Accepting that difficult people work everywhere
Thinking that working with difficult people is rocket science	Recognizing that dealing with people is a skill you can learn, not a matter of luck or fate
Assuming that learning how to work with people isn't important	Focusing on the bottom-line benefits to you and your organization of gaining these skills

01.
WHAT'S WITH ALL THE BITCHING AND MOANING?

How to understand workplace stress.

In the 2006 movie *Crash,* tempers flare. Racial epithets are hurled. Iranian, Korean, black, and white crash into each other, and so do their cultures. The characters all make assumptions about each other. Don Cheadle, who plays an African American detective, reflects on the alienation that is palpable in his world: "It's the sense of touch. In any real city, you walk, you know. You brush past people. People bump into you. In LA, nobody touches you . . . I think we miss that touch so much that we crash into each other just so we can feel something."

It seems like today, wherever you go, people are angry. Rudeness is rampant and it's a rare day when you aren't the target of someone's ire. People snap at you as you order your triple venti, no-foam latte at Starbucks. They're annoyed at how you drive. They get out of bed unhappy and come to work agitated. They take it out on their coworkers, their neighbors, or their spouse. It's a vicious cycle that goes around and around. In this chapter, I am going to help you gain insight into the world of workplace stress.

Why Is Everyone So Crabby at Work?

Yes, most people today are angry about something—and they're wearing that hostility on their sleeves. Moreover, people seem unable to express that anger on their own time. One of the characters in the movie *Crash*, played by Sandra Bullock, expresses her frustration. Her voice cracks as she says, "I'm angry all the time and I don't know why." Unfortunately, the workplace has become a toxic dump for people's annoyances, agitation, and all-out bad behavior. E-mails to my Web site, *www.workplacesthatwork.com*, as well as my audiences' responses tell me that we're facing a virtual epidemic of workplace meanness. Consider these stats:

1. Surveys show that two-thirds of individuals feel burnout on the job.
2. More than half of workers say they work under a great deal of stress.
3. The top source of stress? Difficult coworkers!

It's no surprise that this one-two-three punch creates a triple threat of short tempers, annoyance, and general crabbiness. Just when you're completely burned out, some coworker acts like a jerk.

You probably have your own personal list of people whose behaviors chap your cheeks. It could include loud talkers, screamers, slackers, whiners, gum-smackers, and so much more! The consensus in the March 2006 Randstad survey of 2,318 employed adults on the topic of workplace etiquette (which might be an oxymoron) revealed that:

■ 32 percent of employees listed "loud talkers" as one of their biggest pet peeves in the office.

- 45 percent of those polled said condescending tones were the worst.
- 37 percent found public reprimands at work particularly irritating.

Micromanaging struck a nerve with 34 percent of the respondents, even more than cell phones ringing (30 percent), use of speakerphones in public areas (22 percent), and using PDAs during meetings (9 percent). And 11 percent of those polled hate it when colleagues engage in personal conversations in the workplaces. The Associated Press also collected its own Top Ten List of Annoying Behaviors. Can you believe that some of this stuff really is tolerated? Check it out:

1. The manager who tried to get employees in another department fired for eating bagels that were to be served at a meeting the next day. (My question is, what's up with the manager—day-old bagels?!)
2. The coworker who constantly e-mails the person who is sitting right next to her.
3. The coworker who sits in a crowded cubicle area and puts conversations on speakerphone, including those that detail after-hours exploits better left unexposed.
4. The boss who cuts his fingernails while standing in his employee's cube.
5. The coworker who steals other people's food from the lunchroom refrigerator.
6. The coworker who unilaterally decided to change his job title to look more important.
7. The boss who swears at the top of his lungs and occasionally throws his chair or phone down the hall.
8. The coworker who walks up and randomly scratches other people's backs.

9. The coworker who was caught sleeping on the job more than once and who insisted he was praying every time.

10. The coworker who greeted fellow employees (before the poor souls even had a cup of joe) with the sarcastic welcome, "Are you ready for another fun and *exciting* day?"

I understand workplace woes. I once worked for a brilliant but temperamental manager who habitually yanked his entire phone set out of the wall and threw it across the room. It engendered the post–Cold War duck-and-cover move among his subordinates. I found out recently that on a rare day when he actually used his phone to talk to someone, he called over to the facilities people and asked for a ladder. Anxious to avoid a blowup with the boss, the facilities employee double-timed it to the boss's office. The boss took the ladder from him, climbed up to the top, removed a ceiling tile, and yanked out the intercom system because he was so annoyed at its constant interruptions! This little fit of pique cost the firm $10,000 to repair!

While ripping out the intercom system is an outrageous behavior, it's possible to at least understand the source of it.

What's your limit? When do you say, as the frustrated broadcaster in the movie *Network* urged the world to do, "I'm mad as hell and I'm not going to take it any more?"

Road Rage at Work:
Why There's Hostility in the Hallways

Remember the good old days, when road rage happened only on the freeway? Today, rage has ramped up to include the triggers of cell phones, computers, neighbors, even "disrespecting" looks, say police officers in Milwaukee, where arguments are now the leading cause of homicides. Wow. Simple arguments now end in death. While it's certainly not in the same category as murder, it's not surprising that in poll after poll, Americans say civility is dead. When did good manners die? Perhaps the niceness slide began in the 1990s, when personalities such as Judge Judy, Rush Limbaugh, and Don Imus were given high TV ratings for shaming and taking potshots in the name of entertainment. On cable, commentators including Bill O'Reilly perfected the putdown punch. Reality TV is a barrage of verbal and physical abuse. It's the modern-day matchup between Christians and lions at a Roman circus. Another possible explanation for the increase in behavior that some may consider offensive is the speed of today's communication.

WIRELESS INSOLENCE

Perhaps the wireless tether has people poised for attack. Instant messaging, cell phones, blogs, online shopping, Internet chatrooms, and iPods provide a 24/7 stream of noise, interruptions, multitasking opportunities, and overload. The instantaneous nature of the communication allows us to shoot off an ill-conceived idea, an inflammatory message, a momentary meltdown, or a half-cocked thought without batting an eye. It's too easy.

The problem is, out of the 60,000 or so thoughts we have every day, most are not fit for sharing. We've lost our internal "pause" buttons—all impulse control is out the window! We no longer think *before* speaking or writing. Yet, speak and write we do, burdening others with thousands of lame thoughts, insensitive remarks, and other unsavory unspeakable offenses. Technology has allowed us to broadcast our cheap shots 24/7.

Nancy Ann Jeffrey of *The Wall Street Journal* writes that America's etiquette epidemic may be the "dark side of the New Economy." She opines that boorish behavior is the product of an e-culture that "glorifies speed over decorum and innovation over tradition." It also glorifies communicating before reflecting. Just because we have an enormous number of thoughts every day doesn't mean that anyone else needs or wants to hear them.

Columnist George Will of *The Washington Post* chimes in on the subject, noting that when it comes to pagers, cell phones, text messaging, and video games, children and adults behave the same. "These arrested-development thirteen-year-olds do not distinguish between being in private and being in public. Wherever they are, they are the center of the universe," he writes. Naturally, this culture of rudeness spills into the workplace, making the normal civility that cushions us from the slings and arrows of barbaric behavior a thing of the past.

The Architecture of Annoyance

What's contributing to this souped-up, high-amp culture of annoyance? The very structure of our brain. Yep, the brain is malleable, and we're creating pathways that facilitate rapid response to annoying behaviors. Modern neuroscience is now confirming what ancient yogis knew and taught: The mind is like an untrained monkey, plunging down jungle paths toward bananas and coconuts whether we need them or not.

Unless we train ourselves to pause, and become aware of our feelings, thoughts, and reactions, we will be hijacked by forces beyond our conscious mind all day long. In addition to the five senses of taste, touch, smell, sight, and sound, yogis talked about a sixth sense—thoughts. These include memories and feelings as well as what we usually consider thoughts. With more than

60,000 of these thoughts a day—not to mention the constant sound, smell, and light show from our other senses—we're bombarded. If that weren't enough, we now have an electronic deluge that no other generation has ever experienced. Suddenly, we simply respond to stimuli as if we're part of a Pavlovian experiment; as a society, we're walking around either stupefied or reactive. As both yogis and modern neuroscience have discovered, the same sequence occurs after a thought enters the brain. Each input is first "recognized," and then it is "appraised" or labeled as pleasant, unpleasant, or neutral. Our consciousness then reacts to these stimuli: if pleasant, we react with attraction; if unpleasant, we react with aversion. Then comes the final link: action. If we don't like the stimulus, we push away; if we're attracted, we lunge toward the object of our affection.

Appraisal. Impulse. Action. We go through this triple filter a zillion times a day. It's as though our brains are trapped in a perpetual Xbox Arcade; we're virtually careening through these states and reacting or avoiding all over the machine of life. Unless the mind is finally trained to pause, and we breathe and relax into the stimulus, we simply react without thinking. A radical discovery made by both yogis and modern cognitive therapy is this: We don't have to react. It is possible to experience both pain and pleasure without reacting.

WHAT DOES THAT MEAN TO ME?

What does all this have to do with why everyone is so crabby at work? The constant bombardment of stimuli flung at us by our high-tech, instant gratification world creates a brain on overload. Our brains are simply trying to deal with stimuli as fast as they're coming in, so there's a strong propensity to react without reflection. The brain is trying to cope with a preposterously out-of-control "to-do" list. You know the feeling. You recognize the frustration of always having too many things to do. Naturally, people lash out at coworkers or anyone else who gets in the way.

If you happen to be the recipient of someone else's rage or frustration, it probably makes you want to turn in the opposite direction or strike back. It's the old fight-or-flight choice. It's rare that a person chooses to stand and defuse the situation, creating a more productive outcome and an enriched relationship with a colleague. In upcoming chapters, you'll see how you can control your own part of the interaction, even if others are spinning out of control.

Using the Power of Creative Conflict

The other biggie that causes crabbiness on the job is the Big C: conflict. Most of us hate it, but did you know that we have to have conflict? Most of us don't know why in the world we'd want to have it, or how to deal with conflict appropriately. You can read more about the inherent power of creative conflict and how to embrace it in my book *The Power of a Good Fight: Embracing Conflict to Drive Creativity, Productivity and Innovation.*

The good news is that using conflict productively is a learned skill. You don't have to have natural talent. You don't have to be born with a conflict management gene. Learn the skills; harness the power of creative conflict, and that bitching and moaning will all but disappear. Really. Learn how to have a good fight.

There is absolutely more conflict in most workplaces today than ever before. A more diversified work force, an unbelievably cutthroat competitive environment, rapid technological advancements, international conflict, and the chronic squeeze to do more with less has people pretty worked up. You'd think with all that going on, we'd figure out how to perfect the art of the "good fight." A good fight is one that is:

1. Open, not closed—people admit there's a conflict
2. About ideas, not personalities
3. Where people value the creative potential of conflict
4. Where people skillfully manage their emotions

Sounds like a fight from another planet, doesn't it? Most people have bad fights. Dreadful fights. People are stuck in unproductive battles about personalities, the past, or "beyond" issues—things that are beyond the power of the people in the room to solve, usually structural issues such as budget limitations or lines of authority. These unproductive conflicts cause the combatants to snipe, snarl, and snivel at each other, leading to road rage in the hallways.

ESCAPING THE RAGE TRAP

What is the way out of this trap?

First, people need to realize that conflict is an inevitable part of life. Most conflict originates because we believe that someone or something is just not fair. It's a legitimate observation. Life *isn't* fair. Hence, conflict is inevitable.

Second, most people have not prepared for conflict; they have not created the deep connections with those they work with, nor discussed how they intend to resolve inevitable conflicts when they arise. Most workers have not studied conflict, nor have they practiced the skills of a "good fight" as they would practice if they wanted to improve their game, knit a better sweater, or produce a snappier PowerPoint presentation. You can learn the rules and outcomes if you work on it.

Third, most of us have not realized that all people have a particular "personality style" when they are in conflict. It's the way they respond when they feel pressured, or when their backs are to the wall. Think of your mom when she'd get angry when you were a kid. There was a predictable set of behaviors. You could feel it coming. You knew exactly what your mom was going to do when she reached her limit. Like your mom, most people are creatures of habit. They respond in predictable ways until they get better skills! Changing another person's style is about as easy as convincing a leopard to change her spots, but what you can do is learn how to recognize and work with different styles.

Last, but certainly not least, we need to recognize that most people do not have a deep and abiding purpose in life, one that's wide enough and strong enough to carry them over the rough spots of working through conflicts. Managing conflict is work, and you need to have a higher purpose—a bigger goal that makes it worthwhile to persevere through a difficult conflict.

What's a worried and worked-up worker to do? Never fear. If you plow through the whos, whats, wheres, and whens of this book, you'll know what to do, and why. But first, we need to untangle one preliminary muddle: Who causes all these bad days at work? Is it us, or them?

YOUR RELATIONSHIP TOOLBOX

HOW TO MOVE FROM PISSED OFF TO POWERFUL

PISSED OFF	POWERFUL
Taking others' crankiness personally	Recognizing your own and others' stress
Assuming conflict is dysfunctional	Accepting conflict as a part of every workplace
Ignoring conflict	Learning how to approach conflict proactively and productively
Conflict about personalities	Conflict about ideas

02.
WHAT THE HELL IS YOUR PROBLEM? (MAYBE IT'S YOU)

How to identify whether you or they are the problem.

One summer Saturday night, I was sitting in a café called Wonderview at the top of Coal Creek Canyon, just north of where I live in Golden, Colorado. Suddenly, a 250-pound guy, in a Batman getup, leaped from behind the trailer across the road! He darted in and out of the pines and then evaporated into the cabin behind the trailers, intent upon some secret rescue mission.

"Batman!" I exclaimed. A few diners glanced up and then went back to slurping margaritas and crunching on chips and salsa.

"Oh yeah," my friend muttered. "I've seen him before. He comes out on Saturday nights to entertain people."

"But who is he? What's he doing here?

"Who knows?" My friend, who lives in the canyon and is unfazed by its many eccentric characters, shrugged.

What, Exactly, Does It Mean to Be Difficult?

While longtime canyon residents shrugged off the antics of this would-be Batman as Saturday night entertainment, I was left to ponder how this diverse crowd would handle his eccentric behavior if they knew him in another context. Would the residents of Denver's tonier suburbs tolerate Batman leaping about every Saturday night in their neighborhood? Would it be difficult if he were a part of their family? A neighbor? An employee? A colleague? Is the would-be Batman difficult or just different?

Our decisions about who and what is difficult depends totally on context and our own worldview. Recently, I was talking to one of my colleagues, Bill, about marriage and its many difficulties. "Marriage is hard," he agrees. "Jean has been driving me crazy."

"What does she do?" I asked.

"She's always losing her keys; it drives me nuts!"

Compared to other marital woes, griping about misplaced keys seemed just petty, but to him, it's crazy-making. When I think about the fact that Bill is compulsively organized, I could see that waiting around while Jean searches endlessly for the elusive keys would be beyond maddening.

How about you? Can you tolerate eccentric batmen and missing keys? Do you sweat the small stuff, or do you understand that really, as author Richard Carlson reminded us, it's almost all small stuff? That's not to say that people don't want excellence. Of course, you want to be on a high-performing team. Of course, you want to be surrounded by brilliant, competent people who are also kind and charming and know exactly what to say and when not to speak at all. But, we are on planet Earth, so *stuff happens*. Even if you're surrounded by high-flying extraordinary colleagues, they may drive you nuts! The truth is, that may be more a matter of your own issues—not theirs.

In most workplaces, there *are* truly difficult people who drive everyone batty. Even the Dalai Lama, when pressed on the issue of whether force should be used around the globe, responded in a recent interview that yes, sometimes you do have to use force because there are "rascals afoot in the world." However, whether we see rascals or terrorists may be a matter of our perspective or our place in life.

How do YOU Define Difficult?

How do you decide who is truly difficult? A good test is this: Does the person's behavior have an impact on your individual or team performance? If not, it's eccentric, "rascally" behavior and you need to manage your own attitude. You're not dealing with a truly difficult person who needs to be monitored and managed.

If the person is keeping you from doing your best work, it may be because of what you're doing. Ask yourself if it is because you're engaged in "taking their inventory, not yours," as they say in twelve-step groups. Are you focusing on their faults, instead of spending your energy more productively by improving your own behavior?

SHRUG IT OFF

Sometimes, it's worthwhile to revert to that time-honored teen behavior: the shrug. Pretend for a moment that you are a self-absorbed adolescent, and you'll find that you can simply shrug and look the other way. It'll probably even feel great!

Suppose the shrug is unsuccessful. Suppose that the other person really is keeping you and your team from doing your best work. Assume also that you've done your level best to ignore him or her—to no avail. It's time to get serious about a solution. The first step is diagnosis.

DIAGNOSING DIFFERENCES

This can get dicey. Sometimes, difficult people are some of your best performers. "A" players can be egotistical, demanding, and divisive to morale. Highly intelligent people are often frustrated by those who don't grasp concepts as readily as they do. The difficult person in your department may be a creative type who simply can't conform to a conservative rule-bound workplace, or he or she may simply be in the wrong job. Conversely, *you* might be in the wrong job. If you're in a field that requires a high level of creative energy, but you can't tolerate eccentricity, you may be in the wrong work environment.

For example, one of my executive coaching clients, Bob, came to me about John, one of the junior partners in their high-tech consulting firm. None of Bob's attempts to manage John's idiosyncrasies over the last five years had worked. A software developer, no one could match John's relentless and creative pursuit of the most elegant computer program design, but placing him in front of a new client or other employees led to frequent disaster. John eschewed socks and shirts with collars. He worked all night or not at all, turned up the speakers on his computer to play heavy metal music, and mumbled through presentations. Although frequently late with deadlines, his work was superlative. My frustrated client confessed that John was probably one of the top two or three designers in the world in his subject area.

After coaching from me, Bob finally realized that he needed to restructure his own management style in order to best utilize John. Bob stopped expecting him to meet with clients, gave up on the firm's strict dress code, and softened his approach to office hours. As long as John and the others were producing results, they could work when they liked. They moved John's office to an area where his music annoyed no one.

I did counsel Bob that he would probably always need to closely monitor John to keep him on task. This kind of micromanaging is not worth it for every employee, but for some highly creative and brilliant people it's essential in order to utilize their special gifts.

Who was right here? Should Bob have had to change his own management style and expectations, or should John have "changed his spots" in order to conform to Bob's more conservative and orderly style?

As usual, no one was truly right. Every one of us has our own internal radar, some of which was set at birth; we're genetically loaded to a certain extent to be organized or messy, punctual or distracted, sensitive to others or clueless. This doesn't mean that we can't change, but simply that we come into this world and our bodies (or our Batman costumes) differently. We can either let those differences drive us over the edge, or we can shrug and order another margarita. We can change the environment to accommodate someone's gifts, or we can lose that person to a more accommodating workplace.

Why It's So Hard to Change Other People

Our internal, genetic wiring is like the hardware on a computer. You can change hardware, but it's expensive and time-consuming. This genetic wiring drives much, although not all, of our personality and behavior. Current psychological theoretical consensus is that about 50 percent of our personality and natural behavior is hardwired. The other half is like the software we're running—it's a combination of life experience, training and education, and perhaps, the personal growth, spiritual, or psychological work we've done (or been forced to do) to try to change or evolve.

A MATCH MADE IN WHO-KNOWS-WHERE

One thing I've learned in my numerous years of consulting with conflict-ridden companies is that it's next to impossible to change another person's hardware, and it's also very difficult to get another person to consider running different software.

It's no picnic changing your own either. Part of the problem we have with the "difficult" people in our lives is what psychologists call "matching." In the early days of modern psychology, much of the psychological world was explained by the Freudian belief that it all came down to good mothers and bad mothers. Good moms were able to raise good kids. Bad moms weren't. However, matching theory debunked that notion.

Psychologists now know that much parenting success is simply due to the degree to which parent and child personalities are compatible. A gregarious mom, for example, may be driven batty by an introverted child who is shy, sensitive, and clings to her when confronted by others, regardless of whether those people are friends or strangers. Unless the mom is extraordinarily sensitive and evolved, she will spend her child's life trying to change an introvert into an extrovert.

One of life's greatest challenges is to let the people around us be who they are. This becomes even more difficult if we work with people whose personalities do not match up well with our own. Part of our dilemma also may relate to what psychologist Carl Jung called the shadow. His theory (vastly oversimplified here) is that every person has strengths, or what some call our "light side," and weaknesses, or what he called "the shadow," and what others have called our dark side. Most of us lead with our light side and try to hide, deny, and/or repress our dark side. Frequently, in life, we find ourselves engaged in mirroring, which means that we find others who reflect our own repressed dark side. That reflection is so personally troubling that we respond with annoyance or anger.

What is the solution to this? It's to uncover our own dark and light sides and find healthy ways to express them (such as conversations with friends; therapy; or artistic endeavors), while acknowledging that everyone has dark and light sides, which may simply be a very bad match for ours. If we line up our dark side with someone else's, particularly in a work environment, clashes are utterly predictable.

But, you may protest, the person who is annoying you has totally gone over to the dark side. He has become the Darth Vader of your work group, without a single redeeming quality. I've got to challenge you on that. Even the original Darth Vader from the *Star Wars* movies had his surprisingly good points. He was originally Anakin Skywalker, Luke Skywalker's father, and he was one of the good guys. He went over to the dark side to save Luke's mother, became Darth Vader, forgot who he really was and then, at the end, became good again to save Luke from the evil Emperor Palpatine, but he was mortally wounded and died after gazing upon his son's face for the first and only time.

I must admit that George Lucas' zigs and zags in the series sometimes lost me, but his underlying message rings true: We never know what others have been through in their lives or what they're currently experiencing. Almost every person has goodness within that we can tap if we dig deep enough. Just a glimpse of that can keep us going in our quest to figure out how to work with each person productively.

In rare cases, a matching problem is so bad that there is no choice but to walk away (see Chapter 17). However, this is a last resort and one you shouldn't take until you've tried many, many other solutions! Quitting your job because you don't like your colleagues is an expensive solution—financially, professionally, and emotionally.

Why am I insisting that you try so hard to work with a person you perceive as particularly monstrous? Because every workplace has them. You can keep changing jobs to avoid difficult people, but you never know where they'll pop up again. Learning how to work with challenging people ranks right up there with technical jobs skills. Trust me on this one. You'll use these techniques throughout your working career, no matter on what planet you land.

Difficult People versus Difficult Behavior

Before you can deal with the difficult coworker at your workplace, you need to decide what's difficult. Missing keys? Batmen on the prowl? Is it you or them? It's usually helpful to separate the behavior from the person. It's not your child or your in-laws that you hate (okay, maybe it *is* the in-laws); it's usually a behavior that sends you into fits. Sometimes, people don't even recognize what it is that bugs them about someone. As one of my friends, in the midst of marital discord, wailed, "Even the way he breathes drives me crazy!"

If you've allowed someone else's problem behavior to go on too long, it can push you to the brink of disaster. Not good. This is because it creates a negative spiral of conflict. If you ignore conflict long enough, it spirals down to a very dark place. At that point, you develop what psychologists refer to as "selective perception." Everything someone does drives you nuts at that point. You lose your ability to see the other person as just another struggling human being. Instead, you see him or her as all dark or all light—that "all light" stage is usually called infatuation, while the "all dark" stage has you convinced that your colleague is evil incarnate! If, for example, you're in a long-standing conflict with Joe and you see Mary and Joe chatting together in the hall, who do you assume that they're talking about? You, of course. At this point, you can't even see Joe as a person. Everything he does is suspect.

That's why it's critical to address conflict with coworkers early and often. And of course, with sufficient skill. If you wait too long, the situation becomes nearly intractable. Later chapters in this book will give you a boatload of skills to manage the most difficult kinds of behavior. First, though, we have to answer the essential question of whether it is your stress or theirs that's driving this muddle.

Whose Stress Is It Anyway?

One of the toughest issues is how to decipher whether the "difficult" person is actually creating the problem you're experiencing or whether you are so stressed that the only thing left to do is to blame the difficult person for *your* problem. One simple tool that will help you determine whether you're blaming someone or simply holding him or her accountable is to take the now-famous study from Dr. Thomas H. Holmes and Dr. Richard H. Rahe. The duo created a do-it-yourself stress test.

Banking on the well-documented theory that change causes stress, they examined the stress measured by Life Changes (LCU), ranging from the death of a spouse to receiving a traffic ticket. By adding the LCU values of the past year, you have a rough measure of the likelihood of a stress-related illness or accident, not to mention the odds of crankiness! Using the following list, simply add up the values for the events that have occurred in your life in the last twelve months.

LIFE STRESS	VALUE
Death of a spouse	100
Divorce	73
Marital separation	65
Detention in jail or institution	63
Death of a close family member	63
Major personal injury or illness	53
Marriage	50
Being fired at work	47
Marital reconciliation	45
Retirement	45
Major change in health or behavior of a family member	44
Pregnancy	40
Sexual difficulty	40
Gaining a new family member through birth, adoption, or remarriage	39
Major business readjustment	39
Major change in financial state	38
Death of a close friend	37
Change to a different line of work	36
Major increase in fights with spouse	35
Taking on a mortgage	31
Foreclosure on a mortgage or loan	30
Major change in responsibility at work	30
Son or daughter leaving home	29
In-law troubles	29
Outstanding personal achievement	28
Spouse begins to cease work outside of home	26
Major change in living condition (rebuilding, remodeling)	25
Revision of personal habits	24
Troubles with superior, boss	23
Major change in working hours, conditions	20
Major change in church activities	19
Major change in social activities	18
Purchasing a new car, or other big item	17
Major change in sleeping habits	16
Major change in number of family get-togethers	15
Major change in eating habits	15
Vacation	13
Christmas or holiday observance	12
Minor violations of the law	11

SCORING

BELOW 150 = 30 percent chance of illness or accident within two years

151–299 = 50 percent chance of illness or accident

OVER 300 = 80 percent chance of illness or accident

According to Holmes and Rahe's statistical prediction model, a score of 150 or less means a relatively low (about 30 percent) probability of stress-related illness (including heart attack, cancer, stroke, and so on). A score of 151 to 299 implies a 50 percent probability, and a score of 300 or above implies an 80 percent probability of experiencing a health change—usually a negative change.

Obviously, these predictions are not absolute. Stress and the resulting health problems are the consequence of many different factors, including how significant those life events are to you, your personal resiliencies, and the support available through family, work, and friends. Taking this quiz, however, can give you some insight into the potential risks to your health and well-being. If your score is high on this test, you are likely—unless you're extraordinarily well put together—to be cranky at work! When you're irritable, you can't deal well with anyone, but you are especially at a deficit in dealing with those who get under your skin.

The simple fact is that working with other people remains inherently stressful. In fact, people problems are now the top cause for workplace stress, so you're not alone, according to ComPsych, a Chicago-based employee assistance program. Their StressPlus survey for the second half of 2006 shows 30 percent of those surveyed citing "people issues" as the cause of stress, replacing workload for the first time.

Many people, however, continue to think that work should be stress free. One of my favorite cases is one that a guy in California won in the late 1980s because he claimed he felt uncomfortable at work. In the late 1990s (after a decade of too many silly workplace cases), the same court heard a case from another man who tried to claim that he felt uncomfortable at work. The court said something like: "Get out of here. You're supposed to feel uncomfortable at work. That's why we call it work!"

Before you can begin to decide if it's your coworker who is causing the problem, or it's your own attitude that needs adjusting, you need an accurate assessment of your own stress level. You also need compassion for the stress your coworker may be facing.

An insightful exercise is to take the stress test for someone else. Based upon what you know about the major life events that person has experienced during the past year, where do you believe he or she falls on the stress test levels? If both you and that person are off the charts, you can see how easily collisions can occur.

Ending Bad Days Forever

Ever had a bad day? Perhaps a little too much stress at home, or road rage on the way to work, and then bam, first thing, you run into Mr. Least Favorite employee at the coffee pot, and he has just taken the last cup without making more!

Sometimes, however, we have not just bad days but terrible, horrible days. Days when our coworkers or bosses are engaging in behavior that's not just difficult but over the line into workplace legal or policy violations. How so you know when someone's way out of bounds? The next chapter will help.

YOUR RELATIONSHIP TOOLBOX

HOW TO MOVE FROM PISSED OFF TO POWERFUL	
PISSED OFF	POWERFUL
Finding differences difficult	Analyzing who or what you find difficult
Attacking the person	Separating the person from the behavior
Assuming that others should act like you	Recognizing that many clashes are "matching" problems
Ignoring your stress level	Counting up your own life stress events

03.

YOUR WORKERS' BILL OF RIGHTS

You do know that bra-snapping is not okay, right?

Doris, an HR director at a high-tech company, strolled down a well-lit hallway at work, minding her own business, thinking about the meeting of HR directors she was about to attend. Unbeknownst to her, Ed Idiot, executive vice president of operations, walked behind her. Ed's reputation as a joker in the company preceded him. While some people found his practical jokes hysterical, most employees doubted the sanity of those at the top who had elevated someone with such a sophomoric sense of fun.

As Ed sauntered up behind Doris, he noticed that one of the buttons running down her back was unbuttoned, right where the bra strap ran across her back. To most people, the commonsense options might include continuing to walk to the meeting and politely ignoring the open button, or discreetly telling Doris about the situation. But for reasons that will remain a mystery, Ed regressed to junior high. Yes, he did it: He snapped the bra strap!

I wish I were making this up, but it actually did happen. I was amazed that an EVP of operations didn't understand what was and was not appropriate in the workplace. Sadly, situations such as this still are all too common.

What's Out of Bounds

In this chapter, we'll address behavior that's not just difficult or eccentric, but clearly out of bounds. While who or what you think is difficult can be a matter of your own perspective, as we discussed in Chapter 2, some people travel way over the line. Before you deal with the more subtle kinds of liars, tyrants, and boors, you really need to understand when a colleague's behavior violates company policy, your values, or the law. (I am indebted to Rita Risser for this law/policy/value distinction, and have adapted this discussion with her permission.) If there is a legal or policy violation, you'll have to use one of the techniques in the upcoming chapters to confront the bad actor. If that doesn't work, proceed directly to complaints in Chapter 16.

Understanding Legal, Policy, or Values Violations

When is behavior not just difficult but a violation of law, policy, or your organization's values? It's seems clear that harassing, retaliatory, threatening, or violent behavior is disrespectful, inappropriate, and potentially dangerous. What I've found, however, is that there's confusion about what those terms mean.

KNOW YOUR RIGHTS

Many people seem to believe that anything that offends them, or offends someone they work with, is problem behavior.

Not true. We've had about twenty years' worth of confusion about that in the workplace, resulting in management paranoia, confusing conflicts, and frivolous claims and lawsuits.

It helps to know your rights. One thing I know is that everyone wants to be treated with respect. However, instead of concerning yourself with who is or is not offended by certain behavior in the workplace, consider the following model: Is the behavior a violation of the law, your organization's policy, or your organization's stated values? Believe it or not, there are objective guidelines for what kinds of complaints fit into each of those categories. If behavior doesn't fit in one of those categories but merely happens to be something that offends *you*, you must find a way to negotiate your values. There are many techniques in the following chapters that will help you do just that.

The problem is that because of our increasingly diverse workplace, we're seeing people come into the workplace with conflicting values. Can people with different values work well together? Yes—if they respect the values of those with whom they work without trying to convert them, and if the organization itself has a clear values statement and helps people walk the talk, meaning that they have taken the time to educate people about what those values actually mean.

A Conflict of Values

One of the stranger workplace conflicts I've been called in to resolve involved whether it was appropriate for a woman to take time out of the middle of the day to get her nails done. This was not extra time away from work: She worked long hours and made up the time but the president's secretary did not like her, labeled her as "difficult," and objected to this "off work" time. The Nail Offender's immediate supervisor let her off the hook because she was a good worker. The secretary did not think this was "right," and thus ensued years of petty fighting between the two of them.

Believe it or not, I was called in to negotiate when the conflict had reached the stage at which the two workers refused to speak to each other and their problems interfered with their ability to get work done. Ironically, neither the president of the company nor the HR director wanted to get in the middle of the dispute.

What this boiled down to was a conflict of values. We all have different values. No problem there. The problem comes in when our values are in conflict and the organization has not made it clear where it stands on these values issues. In this case the conflict was over whether it was appropriate to take time off in the middle of the day for an undertaking that appears frivolous to others.

The real weenie here, of course, was the president, who had not made it clear what his (and the organization's) values and polices were about flextime, use of personal time out of the office, and so on. He really thought that everyone should be in the office from 8:00 A.M. to 6:00 P.M. unless they were bleeding, but over time he had succumbed to popular demand for a quasi flextime policy that had merely left everyone confused. The Nail Standoff was simply the symptom of a larger issue— the fact that the company had not explicitly and consistently stated a policy on flextime and workplace hours. Thus, the conflict was beyond the ability of the two employees to solve. The company had to put a stated policy in place.

One way to deal with a values conflict is to analyze the issue and then discuss the clash with the other person or group. (Sometimes, if the situation has gone on too long, you may need a facilitator to accomplish this.) If you can move your own understanding beyond "right" versus "wrong" and recognize that you simply have different values, the situation may become easier to bear. Then it becomes a matter of deciding whether one person's values are in conflict with the organization's stated values. If so, you need to resort to a complaint to a higher authority, as outlined in later chapters. Before doing so, however, I'd caution you to consider that all-important question: "How important is this *really?*" If neither party's values are inconsistent with the organization's stated values, you need to negotiate a resolution of the values clash that you can both live with—perhaps with the help of an intermediary. They are many negotiation and conflict management tips in later chapters of this book.

Illegal Harassment and Discrimination: True Legal Violations

By far the most frequent claim of unacceptable workplace behavior that crosses the legal line remains harassment and/or discrimination. When I wrote my first book on harassment in 1992, I would have assumed that we'd be finished with this topic by now. Unfortunately, that doesn't seem to be the case. Thanks, in part, to bra-snapping EVPs, these claims remain prevalent and real.

But what constitutes illegal harassment and discrimination seems to be the subject of endless workplace confusion. This is because the law sets a floor for your behavior. I call it the "red zone." Most organizations have a policy that is stricter than the law requires. Further, every court in the country has held that companies can have a stricter policy and can discipline people who violate that policy even if the behavior in no way violates the law. Behavior that merely "offends" someone, however, is not a legal problem. Much different standards than that must be met before it qualifies as such.

HARASSMENT AND DISCRIMINATION LEGAL STANDARDS

Federal laws prohibit discrimination, harassment, and retaliation based on:

- Sex or gender
- Age (40 or over; age discrimination)
- Race and color
- Religion
- National origin
- Citizenship
- Physical disability (this may include emotional or mental disabilities)
- Pregnancy
- Veteran/military status
- Family and medical leave

These are often referred to as "protected characteristics." Harassment based on sex includes:

- Sexual harassment
- Gender harassment
- Same-sex harassment
- Harassment based on pregnancy

If you live in California, you have some additional protection. California has perhaps the strictest laws in the country on these issues and also prohibits discrimination, harassment, and retaliation based on:

- Status as domestic violence victim
- Medical condition or genetic characteristic
- Ancestry
- Marital status
- Sexual orientation
- Childbirth and related medical conditions

Many people are confused about the difference between harassment, discrimination, and retaliation. Harassment is not, in fact, based on a new law but is a concept that has been around since the 1964 Civil Rights Act. It is one kind of discrimination.

Discrimination is an adverse job action taken by a supervisor because of the individual's protected characteristics (as explained in the preceding lists). Adverse job actions include failure to hire or promote; firing or a layoff; cuts in pay; a denial of salary increase; and changing other terms or conditions of employment such as hours or vacation time because of a protected characteristic.

Retaliation is an action taken against someone for protesting, complaining, or cooperating in the investigation of discrimination or harassment. This action can include any adverse job action or physical retaliation such as physical threats, assault or battery, destruction of personal property, or stalking.

TYPES OF HARASSMENT

Harassment can be an adverse job action or physical, visual, or verbal action. In the "red zone," there is true illegal harassment, known as *quid pro quo* ("this for that"). This takes the form of "you have to date me to get this job" or "you have to have sex with me to get this promotion." This type of harassment usually involves a colleague or superior leveraging job favors for sexual favors. The harasser is someone who actually has the power to grant such favors, either by express or implied threats. Quid pro quo can also be implied by repeated propositions. As the one who was harassed, you must, however, show that the harassment had some impact on your job; for instance, that you were denied an annual pay increase, laid off, or forced to quit.

Illegal Retaliation

Illegal retaliation is another type of harassment. In this action you are retaliated against by a supervisor, peer, subordinate, or outsiders for refusing sexual advances, for complaining about harassment or discrimination, or assisting in a claim. This retaliation can take many forms, such as demotion, poor performance appraisals, bad job assignments, termination, threats, or violence.

For example, one investigation I was asked to conduct on a retaliation claim involved an employee at a high-tech company. He alleged that he was retaliated against because he had testified as a witness in a racial discrimination case. He claimed that the VP involved in the case "belittled" him in meetings after he testified. While this might have been a good claim of retaliation, my investigation revealed that this particular VP treated other employees exactly the same way and that the employee himself had been treated in the same manner *before* the lawsuit.

Sexual Favoritism

Another type of illegal harassment is illegal sexual favoritism. If it's isolated instances of management giving favorable treatment to paramours, in most cases it isn't illegal, although it probably violates your organization's policy. It is illegal if sexual favoritism is widespread in the company.

HOSTILE ENVIRONMENT

Last, but not least, is an illegal hostile environment. This is the accusation that many people hurl around carelessly. Many people seem to think that they are in a hostile environment if someone's behavior offends them. Not true. In order to prove a true hostile environment you have to show that the behavior was discriminating or sexually harassing in tone and nature. This means that it was based on one of the protected characteristics listed earlier. In other words, it's not just that someone is harassing you, but that he or she is harassing you specifically because of your sex, race, color, religion, and so on. Contrary to popular belief, in most states, there's no such thing as illegal "general" harassment. If it's not tied to one of these protected classifications, it is not illegal. However, general harassment may violate criminal laws (assault, stalking, and threats among them) if it is severe enough.

Second, you must prove that the behavior is unwelcome by the victim, meaning that you didn't encourage the behavior or participate in it. Third, in order to prove illegal harassment, you must show that it was severe, meaning that it interfered with work. Last, you have to prove that the employer knew about the harassment, or should have known, and did nothing. You must be able to prove all four of these factors in order to prove illegal harassment under the law.

Harassment or Discrimination Under Your Organization's Policies

Employers can, and frequently do, prohibit all harassment under their own policies, not just harassment based on race, sex, or other protected characteristics. This may include all behavior that is disrespectful. Check your organization's policies, which should be posted in the workplace or on the Web site. You may be surprised to learn how broad it is. A typical statement might be:

WORKPLACE HARASSMENT

ABC Company is committed to providing all employees with a work environment free from hostility and harassment and provides this policy to express that commitment. We recognize that harassment of employees in any form destroys morale, impairs productivity, and is not permissible in a productive, cooperative environment.

ABC Company will carefully investigate and vigorously enforce all reported violations of this policy. Harassment by management or coworkers including but not limited to harassment based upon race, sex, color, religion, national origin, age, disability, or veteran status, whether verbally or physically, will not be tolerated. Harassing language or actions are not only a violation of company policy, but may constitute an illegal act. We will comply with all federal, state, and/or local laws.

ABC Company prohibits workplace harassment of every kind, including sexually related conduct of a physical, verbal, or visual nature that creates an intimidating, hostile, seductive, or offensive work environment; unwanted touching, patting, grabbing, repeated objectionable sexual flirtations, propositions, suggestive comments, lewd jokes, and display in the workplace of sexually explicit objects, drawings or photos. Of course, ABC Company also prohibits any employee from making unwelcome sexual advances or requests for sexual favors when submission or rejection of such conduct is used as the basis for employment-related decisions.

Statements that said employer prohibits harassment "in any form" have become quite common in most workplaces. These statements can provide you with powerful ammunition when you confront the person whose boorish behavior may be borderline harassment and/or when you need to talk to your manager or HR.

If you're still confused about what really crosses the line into legal or policy violations, check out the following list, provided by one of my clients:

Examples of Legal or Policy Violations

- Objectionable comments about a person's age, race, skin color, national origin, ethnic background, religion, gender, marital status, disability or medical problem, or veteran status
- Repeated and unwelcome requests for a date
- Racial, sexual orientation, sexist, age-related, or sexual jokes or comments
- Referring to a coworker in demeaning language (babe, girl/ boy, broad, colored, cripple, grandpa, pops)
- Following a person inside or outside of work
- Making sexual gestures
- Wearing or displaying the Confederate flag
- Accessing or displaying sexual or racial pictures, cartoons, or Web sites
- Unwelcoming touching of a person's hair, clothing, or body
- Unwelcome kissing, hugging, or patting
- Wearing or displaying hate-related symbols (e.g., a swastika)
- Restraining or blocking the path of a person
- Touching oneself in a way that is suggestive in view of a coworker
- Spreading rumors about a coworker's sex life, including affairs, marital status, or sexual orientation

- Repeatedly leering at a coworker
- Making sexually suggestive facial expressions (winking, blowing kisses)
- Treating someone differently after a legally protected medical or family leave
- Neglecting to consider a woman with small children for a job that requires travel
- Refusing to consider an older applicant because he or she is "over-qualified"

NOTE: This list of examples does not include all potential legal or policy violations.

There is always a question, of course, of whether your organization is willing to enforce the law and their policies. There is also the personal issue of whether you want to raise this with anyone for fear of formal or informal retaliation. We'll deal more fully with those issues in Chapter 16.

Values Violations

In addition to formal policy statements, many organizations also have values statements. While these may seem as familiar and useless as wallpaper, you would be well advised to check them out, read them, and ponder whether any of the behavior you're receiving at work seems to violate the organization's stated values. These values may include things such as "people are our most important resource" and "we respect all our employees."

Although it's easy to become cynical about whether the organization really stands behind and intends to enforce these messages, if you bring them up at the appropriate time (more about this in later chapters), such as when you're talking to the person engaging in the problem behavior or your manager or HR, it can be an incredibly skillful move. What I'm suggesting here is something along the lines of "Ed Idiot is doing X. When I was thinking about X, I started wondering if X were consistent with our values as a company. In looking at our statement of values in our policy manual, I see that we say Y. It just doesn't seem to me that Ed Idiot's behavior is consistent with our company values. Could you please clarify for me what is acceptable under our values statements?"

Other Workplace Legal Issues

Other examples of clearly illegal behavior in the workplace include issues such as your supervisor denying you legitimate breaks or overtime if you're an hourly worker; failing to allow you appropriate time off under the Family and Medical Leave Act; disability discrimination and/or failing to allow appropriate accommodations if you have a disability; or denying workers' compensation, whistleblower protection, or privacy. This chapter deals only with some of the more common violations.

HOURLY VERSUS EXEMPT QUALIFICATIONS

In order to establish whether you are in fact entitled to overtime, you must first know whether or not you are an exempt or hourly employee. If you are exempt, what exactly are you exempt from? Being paid overtime. If you do not have significant supervisory responsibilities and/or high-level administrative or technical expertise, you're hourly. You have a right to be paid overtime.

FAILURE TO ALLOW FAMILY AND MEDICAL LEAVE

You have a right to twelve weeks a year of unpaid leave after your first year of employment to take care of a serious health condition, whether it's your own or that of an immediate family member. Being denied this is illegal under the Family and Medical Leave Act (FMLA). You do not need to take this time off all at once but can do it in increments, as long as the total is no more than twelve weeks per year.

DISABILITY

If you have what the federal Americans with Disabilities Act (ADA) qualifies as a "permanent and substantial impairment of a major life function," your employer can't discriminate and must accommodate you.

What is a *major life function*? Generally, the term encompasses things such as working, eating, sleeping, and walking. Could sex qualify as a major life function, meaning that you would be considered disabled if you couldn't have sex? Believe it or not, the U.S. Supreme Court had to consider just such a case.

A truck driver hurt his back. He could still drive a truck, so he couldn't claim that as a permanent impairment of a major life function; he claimed instead that the back injury affected his sex life. He argued that before he hurt his back he was able to have sex thirty or forty times a month but after the injury, he could only have sex three to four times per month. The court said that it did not believe that sex was a "major life function" such that he was disabled. They also pointed out that he had introduced no evidence of being able to have sex so often.

If you are still able to perform your job and your employer can reasonably accommodate you without undue hardship, you have the right to be accommodated. Accommodations may include a special screen for your computer, a special chair because of back problems, or a flexible schedule for doctor's appointments. Time off may also be appropriate. If disabled, you may not be denied a promotion or job if you are able to the work with a reasonable accommodation.

WHISTLEBLOWER PROTECTION

You can't be fired or disciplined for reporting a violation of the law or for refusing to violate a law. One of the first whistleblower cases involved a man who was called to testify against his employer in an IRS case. His boss came in the day before he was scheduled to testify and said the man should lie when he testified in court the next day because if he told the truth they would lose. The employee said that he couldn't lie because he would be under oath. The boss replied that he could do what he liked but "I'm just telling you: tell the truth and you'll be fired!"

Sure enough, the employee told the truth and they canned him. When he sued, the court found that it was the public policy of the state of California (and every other state) for people to be able to tell the truth in court and not be fired for doing so. This became known as whistleblower protection. Several different federal statutes, in addition to court cases, protect your right to complain about legal or public policy violations in the workplace, as well as to refuse to violate the law.

WRONGFUL TERMINATION AND OTHER WRONGFUL ACTIONS

Believe it or not, the law implies that in employment relationships, you have a right to be treated fairly, as long as you are performing your duties and responsibilities as an employee in a reasonable way. This has been interpreted to mean that you should be warned before you're fired, be given the promotions you were promised, and be treated fairly and in good faith.

Let me give you an example of one of the first cases in the country that considered this idea. It was a case brought by a gentleman named Wayne Pugh against See's Candies, Inc. Mr. Pugh started out working at See's as a dishwasher. Over the course of his thirty-two-year career, he worked his way up to vice president in charge of production.

Over time, Mr. Pugh and the president of the company became friends; they, and their spouses, even traveled and socialized together. The four had just returned from a golfing vacation in Spain. The day after the trip Mr. Pugh walked into the president's office and the president abruptly fired him. When Mr. Pugh asked why, the president simply responded, "Look deep within your heart and you will find the answer." No other explanation was offered. Mr. Pugh looked deep within his heart, found the name of an attorney, and sued! He won the case. The court said that it was a violation of the "covenant of good faith and fair dealing" to fire a long-term employee with no warning.

PRIVACY VIOLATIONS

You have a right to keep your private life private at work. Inappropriate or unwelcome questions about your personal life, medical issues, or off-work activities could violate your privacy. You have a right, for example, to march in a KKK parade or a gay rights rally on your non-work time. Even if your employer finds out about these activities and disapproves, in most states you cannot be fired, disciplined, or harassed because of these non-work-hours pursuits.

Threats and Violence

You have a right to be safe at work. If someone's threatening physical harm or engaging in physical abuse at work, they're violating the law, as well as, most likely, your employer's policy. Most organizations have strong statements against threats and violence. Here is an example:

> "Every employee has a strong interest and responsibility in helping to maintain a safe working environment for themselves and their coworkers. The company strives to ensure a safe environment for all employees, and this policy is issued and administered to support this commitment.
>
> The company and its employees will have zero tolerance for threats and violent acts in the workplace. Examples of this could include intimidating, threatening or hostile behaviors such as physical abuse, vandalism, arson, sabotage, use of weapons, carrying weapons onto company property, or any other act which in management's opinion is inappropriate to the workplace. Employees who observe or have knowledge of any violation of this policy should immediately report it to company management, human resources or corporate security, and should directly contact proper law enforcement authorities if there is an immediate serious threat to the safety or health of themselves or others."

Every case of workplace violence by employees has been thoroughly studied. The vast majority of perpetrators had long years of service with their companies. Usually they felt they had been denied a promotion they thought they were entitled to, or they had been terminated. In virtually every case, the perpetrators made threats beforehand.

Most people who are violent share characteristic behaviors and exhibit warning signs. If you see a number of the following signs (not just one) you need to complain to your manager or HR department immediately:

- Threatening and Disturbing Behavior
  - *Direct and indirect threats*
  - *Mood swings, depression, bizarre statements, delusions of persecution*
- History of Violence
  - *Domestic violence, verbal abuse, antisocial activities*
- Romantic Obsession
  - *Physical or romantic obsession*
- Substance Abuse
  - *Trouble with alcohol or drug addiction*
- Depressive Behavior
  - *Self-destructive behavior*
  - *Loner behavior or isolating themselves from others*
  - *Unkempt physical appearance, despair, sluggish decision-making*
- Pathological Blamer
  - *Accepts no responsibility for his or her actions*
  - *Constantly blames coworkers, employer, the system*
- Impaired Ability to Function
  - *Poor impulse control*
- Obsession with Weapons
  - *Ownership of gun or gun collection, combined with antisocial behavior*
  - *Fascination with shooting skills or weapon-related activity*
- Personality Disorder
  - *Antisocial or borderline personality disorders*

- *Irritable, aggressive, involved in disputes or fights with others*
- *May steal or destroy property with little remorse*
- *Borderline personality shows moodiness, instability, impulsive action, easily agitated*

More detail on the legal problems discussed in this chapter is beyond the scope of this book, although many valuable resources are listed in the appendices. Note, also, that some of these laws only apply if your organization has a certain number of employees. The number varies by the particular law but could be from fifteen to fifty. What's important is to recognize when someone has crossed the line from merely difficult to doing something illegal or acting in a way that is clearly a violation of your organization's policy or values. These situations require an approach that is different from the one you would take when dealing with generic liars, tyrants, and boors.

Now that you've had a chance to ponder *what* behavior you find difficult, you may be wondering how to connect with these rascals. I'll solve that mystery in the next chapter.

YOUR RELATIONSHIP TOOLBOX

HOW TO MOVE FROM PISSED OFF TO POWERFUL

PISSED OFF	POWERFUL
Tolerating behavior that's clearly out of bounds	Recognizing when someone's behavior isn't just difficult but illegal
Ignorance of your organization's policies and the law	Understanding your rights
Dismissing the warning signs of violence	Knowing the warning signs of violence
Whining to your friends about truly bad behavior	Complaining to your manager or HR if you believe someone is violating the law or policy

04.

HOW TO CONNECT EVEN WHEN YOU DON'T WANT TO

Get by with a little help from your friends.

In the casting call for bozo bosses, Jerry rates number one on Pam's list. Rumor has it that Jerry is the vice president of human resources. Reality would suggest otherwise. It would seem that Jerry's preferred role is R.A.W., otherwise known as "Retired-at-Work." Counting the days until his retirement, Jerry avoids starting anything new that might require real work, be considered controversial, or demand attention to delicate details. He keeps all the tried-and-true approaches on track, running on autopilot as much as possible. Jerry is completely ho-hum. He's not causing enough visible trouble to raise eyebrows, but he's creating enough believable bureaucracy to thwart every innovative solution that Pam offers. Innovation is just too much trouble.

You probably know people like Jerry. If your coworkers are disengaged, you will experience feelings of loneliness, frustration, and anger on the job. Moreover, if you feel that you are one of the few actually doing the work, you'll join the ranks of your disengaged and apathetic colleagues overnight. The solution to this annoying and common problem is one word: connection.

For Love or Money?

Most of us spend more time at work than we do with our families. People need to feel connected at their workplace—money alone is never enough to keep talented people. Connections within teams, among departments, and to trade organizations and professional associations all matter. Feeling connected lowers stress. It increases retention. If you feel tightly linked to people at work, you're likelier to be more productive and more satisfied. On the other hand, if you feel separated, if you feel invisible, or if you just don't click with people, you're probably going to feel higher stress and will burn out faster than you would otherwise. What does this have to do with working with difficult people? A lot. If you connect before the difficulty—the ideal scenario—you'll be less likely to have trouble. Also, working through difficulties and challenging relationships requires motivation. This chapter will help give you the push you need.

Why You Should Connect with People You Can't Stand

Although we can't change people's hardwiring, we can influence their behavior. If you doubt this, consider for a moment this mind-boggling research about particle physics found at *http://www.nist.gov/public_affairs/images/NIST_CatStates_embed.html.* The National Institute of Standards and Technology uses a clever animation to demonstrate an amazing phenomenon. It shows six separate ions, each spinning in two opposite directions at the same time, called a superposition. An animated laser beam hits one of the particles, and the superposition collapses. Then, all the particles immediately start to spin in the same direction.

In the spooky science of entanglement, measuring only one of them sets the direction of spin for all of them!

This sort of connection between particles—in which reality is changed by measurement—has been talked about since Einstein's day, and it has been seen experimentally in pairs of photons for decades. We may not be able to directly extrapolate between physics and people. However, many scientists assert that the spinning particles theory tells us something that many of us know instinctively: We can influence the behavior of others simply by how we behave, feel, and think in the workplace, our very "beingness." *The workplace environment isn't something that just happens around you; your very presence there influences it.* When you step into a river, the very act of putting your foot in it changes the current. So, too, does your presence influence the tone of your workplace. When you become conscious of that, you realize that you can influence the way everyone spins. There's no need for everyone to spin unconsciously in the wrong direction. By being aware, you influence the way the entire team spins.

Why Bother to Connect?

What's the big upside of connecting? Well, as Edward Hallowell's book *Connect* tells us, we literally connect or we die. Hallowell, a psychiatrist and Attention Deficit Disorder expert, managed a successful psychiatric practice outside Boston. His clients were mainly successful male corporate executives. He noticed that, over time, the problems his clients discussed changed. Previously, clients struggled with troubled marriages or out-of-control teens, but then clients began flocking to him with clinical depression. These were men who had all the trappings of success: outstanding careers with impressive titles, mansions to match, second homes, sports cars, member-ships in prestigious organizations and clubs—the works. Hal-lowell began researching the cause of their depression. Most of Hallowell's clients gave him some version of the following: "I used to spend my days connecting with people, mentoring them, coaching them, and leading meetings. Now I spend my days staring at a computer screen."

Hallowell started studying some of the research on mon-keys and on babies who were in orphanages. These beings actually died if they didn't receive enough human connection. Similarly, he found that our screen-obsessed society is heading for disaster. The human brain is wired to connect with other humans and animals. If humans don't receive enough of those feel-good chemicals that are fueled by intimacy, they become depressed. If the void is so vast and there is so little connection, we die. We simply lose the ability and will to sustain life. We respond just like the babies and monkeys who did not receive enough attention or physical touch.

If you doubt that we're wired for connection, check out brain-science writer Daniel Goleman's book *Social Intelligence*. Goleman explains, "Our brain has been preset for kindness. We automatically go to the aid of a child who is screaming in terror; we automatically want to hug a smiling baby. Such emotional impulses are "prepotent;" they elicit reactions in us that are unpremeditated and instantaneous. That this flow from empathy to action occurs with such rapid automaticity hints at circuitry dedicated to this very sequence. To feel dis-tress stirs an urge to help. When we hear an anguished scream, it activates the same parts of our brain that experience such anguish, as well as the premotor cortex, a sign that we are pre-paring to act. Similarly, hearing someone tell an unhappy story in doleful tones activates our motor cortex—which guides movements—as well as the amygdala and related circuits for sadness. This shared state then signals the motor area of the brain, where we prepare our response, for the relevant action. Our initial perception prepares us for action: to see readies us to do."

None other than Charles Darwin anticipated this hardwiring. He postulated that empathy was a survival mechanism. Those who connected well with others were more likely to survive because they had the help and support of the tribe. We are literally the ancestors of good connectors.

"For instance," Goleman continues, "when we see someone expressing fear—even if only in the way they move or hold their body—our own brain activates the circuitry for fear. Along with this instantaneous contagion, the brain areas that prepare for fearful actions also activate, and so on with each emotion—anger, joy, sadness. Emotional contagion then does more than merely spread feelings—it automatically prepares the brain for appropriate action."

Ironically, our strongest sympathetic reaction is to fear. Again, think back to the tribe. If one person saw someone expressing fear in the tribe, it was enough to set the entire tribe running to escape the terrible tiger that was sure to follow. This "emotional contagion" had both a survival and biological imperative.

As Goleman explains, "If the human brain contains a system designed to attune us to someone else's distress and prepare us to act to help, then why don't we always help? The possible answers are manifold, enumerated by countless experiments in social psychology. But, the simplest answer may be that modern life militates against it: We largely relate to those in need at a distance. That separation means we experience "cognitive" empathy rather than the immediacy of direct emotional contagion. Or worse, we have mere sympathy, where we feel sorry for the person but do not taste their distress in the least. This more removed relationship weakens the innate impulse to help."

As neuroscientist Stephanie Preston and biologist Frans de Waal note, "in today's era of e-mail, commuting, frequent moves, and bedroom communities, the scales are increasingly tipped against the automatic and accurate perception of others' emotional state, without which empathy is impossible." We experience others at a distance, what I call "secondhand lives." What we see on the TV screen may seem more real to us than our sick neighbor down the block or a colleague who needs our help.

Why Connections at Work Matter

What does all this brain science do to help the relationship-impaired among us connect? For one thing, it helps us see that we've been wired for connection and community ever since we spent our time sitting around our communal campfires and then crawled out of the cave. Indeed, physical anthropologists tell us that we were selected for connection. Those who learned how to connect were more likely to survive in the jungle or the desert; if our ancestors banded together they were less likely to be killed by lions or tigers or bears.

If we band together, our company is more likely to outlast the competition. Our organization is more able to accommodate a rapidly changing environment if the team is connected. Global competition, issues around sustainable growth, terrorism, and even road rage may seem more abstract, but the truth remains. At a basic level, if we want to survive and if we want to ward off significant depression, we need to connect. Our sensitive brains demand it. Connecting at work really is part of our biological imperative. Because of that, connecting with the everyday bozos and boors is still in some ways a primal part of survival. If you remember that you are part of a species born to connect, you can find empathy and bridge differences more easily.

Most U.S. Workers Are Disconnected

Recent polls reveal that most organizations fail at the task of keeping workers connected to either the organization or their coworkers. A Gallup poll, for example, reveals that only 26 percent of U.S. employees are fully engaged at any time. On the other end of the spectrum, 19 percent of employees are actively disengaged, meaning they intentionally act in ways that negatively impact their organizations. The annual cost to employers of this actively disengaged group exceeds $300 billion nationwide. (This does, of course, prompt one to wonder: what's up with all those folks in the middle? *"Comfortably numb,"* perhaps, as the Pink Floyd song goes?)

Clearly, we're now able to document the existence of high-involvement, high-wage, high-profit companies in almost every industry—for example, Southwest Airlines; Nucor Corporation; W.L. Gore & Associates; Xilinx, Inc.; Harley-Davidson, Inc.; UPS; Costco Wholesale Corporation; Starbucks; and Alcoa, Inc., to cite just a few. These productive and growing companies also have lower labor costs overall than do their low-wage competitors. How? They ensure that workers participate in decision-making, reward employees fairly for their efforts, and provide them with good training and career opportunities. Their employees reciprocate the favor in terms of much higher productivity than that of workers in comparable low-wage companies. Starbucks executives, for example, explain that they're able to offer unusually high benefits to their employees not because they charge a premium for their product, but because their productive, customer-sensitive employees allow the company to realize a premium for the products and services they offer. My client Southwest Airlines, for example, walks this talk. I had a highly personal experience of just how committed their founder and former C.E.O., Herb Kelleher, is to employee engagement when I spoke to 200 of the company's top executives. My client contact introduced me to Herb, who complimented me on the presentation and was scheduled to have lunch with me. Herb and I started to walk across the meeting room to the buffet table together. Actually, I should say I walked; Herb gabbed. He stopped to talk to every single person along the way—and not just a quick hello, but long discussions of each person's recent birthday, new grandchild, divorce, or whatever was going on in each employee's life. After that, I never doubted that most of his employees would walk through fire for him.

How to Connect

Even if your organization fails to join the employee engagement bandwagon, you can launch your own connection campaign. Connecting with people makes it easier to affect their behavior. Connecting with people before things blow up makes the inevitable conflicts easier to resolve. So, there's clearly a self-serving reason to connect with boors and bozos. It really is worth the trouble! With a few pointers, even the relationship-impaired can connect. I'll offer many more ideas throughout this book, but here are a few to get you started:

1. **Start connections early and often**: Invite newcomers for coffee, lunch, or a walk. If your new colleague is of

the opposite gender, invite a few people so that your noble intentions are abundantly clear. Getting to know people at a personal level before they start to annoy you always helps.

2. **Learn to listen well.** In our ADD age, just having someone's full attention is a gift. Even five minutes of undivided attention from someone can lead to more positive interactions. Don't multitask!

3. **Cultivate compassion.** If we try to empathize with what the other person is feeling, we help create connection. Try to remember a time in your own life when you had similar feelings or thoughts. As psychiatrist Daniel Stern explains, our nervous systems "are constructed to be captured by the nervous systems of others, so that we can experience others as if from within their skin."

4. **Relate those similar feelings and thoughts.** This helps the other person resonate with your brain. This defines rapport. Rapport includes mutual attention, shared positive feelings, and physical mirroring.

5. **Celebrate.** This helps set up the shared positive feelings part of rapport. Take it upon yourself to create small celebrations for completing a sale or a new project and for marking milestones such as a new baby, engagement, or birthday. Bonding during happy times helps us through the sad times.

6. **Understand unwritten rules.** Every family, work group, and society has them. There are secrets that we don't tell grandmother, for example, or generic-looking coffee cups that, in fact, belong to the boss. Some people understand these rules and ferret them out instinctively, but just knowing they exist can help. Ask someone for help in decoding the unwritten rules when you're new

to an organization. Similarly, you might consider giving a new coworker a discreet "heads-up" if you anticipate he or she may commit a faux pas.

7. **Learn to read others accurately.** Many of us know how to do this instinctively. This includes the art of reading others' nonverbal cues. For example, if you've ever tried to talk to someone who thought that standing with his back to you while talking was appropriate, you know what I mean. If you aren't naturally good at reading between the lines, take heart. You're not alone. There's actually a name for the inability to read social cues. It's called dyssemia, and there are books and programs that can help. (See Paul Ekman, Micro Expression Training Tool [METT] in Appendix A of this book.)

8. **Learn the art of presentation and persuasion.** It's one thing to understand how someone feels; it's another to act appropriately on that knowledge. It can be done, however. Books and seminars abound on this subject. Take advantage of the information age.

9. **Repeat often: We're all doing the best we can.** There are no perfect workers, mates, parents, or children. We're all, to a greater or lesser extent, the victim of our history, our brain chemistry, our unhealed wounds, and our childhood. Despite this, the majority of people are trying to connect, to be kind, to do the right thing. We're not always perfect, and we're not always kind, but we need to acknowledge our shortcomings when we can. As pioneering behavioral psychologist B. F. Skinner taught us, what is reinforced gets repeated. Anytime someone demonstrates a kind, connecting act toward you, express your appreciation in words and deeds. This acknowledgment reinforces the act and makes it more likely to recur. Do your part.

EMPTY YOUR EMOTIONAL TRASH

Author Laurel Mellon argues that before people can even form a connection, each has to clear out "emotional trash," old issues that interfere with the ability to have a clear connection with another person. As the pioneering psychologist Carl Rogers explained, "The curious paradox is that when I can accept myself just as I am, then I can change."

How do you do this? One way is to more often notice what we're feeling, be honest with ourselves, and allow feelings to run their course. Psychologist Gay Hendricks offers this explanation from his book *Conscious Living: Finding Joy in the Real World*:

"Accepting yourself begins with fundamentals such as letting yourself feel your emotions to completion. What does this mean? If you begin feeling sad, for example, when you are watching a movie, it's likely that the movie is touching an issue of your own. Instead of rushing out of the movie back into your busy life, let yourself feel the emotions that were stirred into motion by the scene in the film. The paradox of awareness is that if you give yourself full permission to feel your emotions, you don't find yourself stuck in the unsettling grip of them."

For most of us, everyday workplace interactions bring up lots of emotions, which may remind us of old unhealed memories or hurts. While it's painful and unsettling, we need to feel those emotions deeply in order to connect more deeply with our coworkers as well as ourselves and others in our lives. This is neither an easy task, nor one for the faint of heart. But, as Desmond Tutu points out, there's nothing else that can save our troubled world.

You may be whining at this point that all this connecting is a lot of hard work. Gaining an attitude adjustment is the first step. Once you've mastered your own reasons and motivations for understanding the liars and tyrants and boors among us, you're better able to cope with the effort that requires. As you'll learn in Chapter 5, understanding *why* people do what they do can give us the will and the reason to connect.

YOUR
RELATIONSHIP TOOLBOX

HOW TO MOVE FROM PISSED OFF TO POWERFUL	
PISSED OFF	POWERFUL
Believing that you can ignore coworkers	Understanding that connecting with others is a biological imperative
Ignoring difficult people without even trying to connect	Understanding that difficult coworkers will be easier if we create connections
Assuming connecting is difficult	Taking small steps to connect with new people
Assuming lack of connection is the other person's fault	Recognizing that our inability to connect may be the result of our own "emotional trash"

05.
ARE THEY DOING IT JUST TO PISS YOU OFF?

How to understand how people are hardwired.

Jerry McGruder is going nuts. The young twentysomethings he has hired show up for work with tiny earbuds pumping music or cell phone conversations into their ears—and they wear collarless shirts and tennis shoes to the office. More often than not they look like they've hopped out of bed, thrown on a pair of jeans, and forgotten to comb their hair! Jerry sighs when he looks at them.

When he tries to shake hands, they seem unsure of what the custom is. However, they bombard him with a relentless flurry of e-mail, text, and instant messages—even when sitting in a cubicle less than twenty feet from Jerry's door! "Why can't they walk in and talk to me?" Jerry fumes. "Don't they know how to carry on a professional conversation?"

When he mentions his favorite TV show, they look at him blankly. "And what is the X in the Xbox?" he asks. Work never used to anger him this much, he confides to his wife at dinner in the evening.

Diversity: It Ain't Love at First Sight

In my experience, while each situation is unique, there are two big overlooked reasons why people in the workplace can seem impossibly difficult to you:

- Unacknowledged and unresolved diversity issues
- Unrecognized (and frequently untreated) mental health issues

Let's deal with diversity first.

When someone you work with drives you batty, it helps to consider whether there are generational, cultural, or ethnic differences that may be contributing to the clashes. Consider these stats:

- By 2010, almost 70 percent of the new entrants into the U.S. workforce will be women and people of color. By 2020, more than 50 percent of workers will be older than fifty years old.
- In 2003, 53.7 percent of all mothers with infants were involved in the labor force, up from 31 percent in 1976.
- According to the U.S. Census Bureau projections, in less than fifty years, immigration will cause the population of the U.S. to increase from its present 288 million to more than 400 million.

And consider the explosive movement of U.S. jobs to India and China. In April 2006, for example, Google announced a Chinese-language brand name for its search engine: GU Ge, or "harvesting song." However, Google found that many new hires, accustomed to following explicit instructions, had a hard time with Western management style, in which it is common to confront a boss, and seizing the initiative without specific direction is embraced. To help East meet West, Google is trying out new Internet-based training and team-building exercises, sometimes even before new hires begin work. The company is also recruiting mentors. It's finding Mandarin-speaking experts skilled in the ways of Western research and development to advise new employees and assist them with the transition to a work life that is different from anything they've ever known.

Generation X, Y, and MySpace?

Generation X is the generation that followed the baby boomers. The X'ers were born between 1965 and 1976 or so, depending on whose research you follow. They have been defined by the media as a group vastly different from the intense, hard-working boomers. Deserved or not, the X'ers have acquired the labels of slackers, more interested in having personal time than in going the extra mile to win a promotion. They value independence, technology, and informality. They were the original latchkey kids and the first group to experience MTV.

Any generation is more than a demographic chart, and the X'ers are no exception. They are the most diverse generation in history. According to the U.S. Census, about a third of them are nonwhite or Hispanic. Most of them grew up after the Civil Rights movement and thus tend to be more tolerant of differences among people.

The generation that is following the X'ers is young, brash, and just hitting the work force. Anyone born in 1977 or after is considered part of the Y Generation, but some demographers consider the back end to be 1989, while others say it's as late as 2002.

Following closely on the heels of the Y Generation is the cohort recently dubbed by *Newsweek* as the "MySpace" generation—based on the popular online social networking site. Like their older Generation Y and X siblings, they are great multitaskers—adept at moving from phone to video to computer games to instant messaging, sometimes all at once. These generational groups are also willing and wanting to question the status quo. They push back against parents, and they do the same with employers. They've grown up with constant consultations about what they think and feel, in the classroom and at home. Employers, who don't readily embrace that practice, find themselves on the receiving end of blank stares at best, and, at worst, outright or passive-aggressive rebellion.

How should you deal with these iPod-toting technical wizards (especially when you want to strangle them with their headphone cords)? Communication is key—but recognize that generations communicate differently. As a colleague or manager, you need to understand and work within that framework if you want results.

Talking with the Enemy

Experts report that there is more information in the daily *New York Times* than someone born in the 1700s knew in an entire lifetime. Instead of poring through library stacks, students can Google what they need in an instant. They may have access to more information than ever before, but they often don't have the time or the wisdom to make sense of the data deluge.

Also, consider the younger generation's frame of reference. The Beloit College Mindset List, released by humanities professor Tom McBride and public-affairs director Ron Nief, is an annual catalog of seventy-five cultural landmarks that give us some perspective on how the current freshman class views the world. Check out these examples from the list:

- "They have known only two presidents."
- "The Soviet Union has never existed and therefore is about as scary as the student union."
- "Carbon copies are oddities found in their grandparents' attics."
- "Reality shows have always been on television."
- "Madden has always been a game, not a Super Bowl winning coach."

And of course, they're the instant- and text-messaging champs. The key question among responsible colleagues is when and when not to use these methods of communication. Ask people from different generations and you're likely to get different answers.

The recent crop of college grads, those born in the early 1980s, have brought with them a set of technological tools that make fax machines, voice mail, and spreadsheet software look positively quaint. They've grown up with scanning, text messaging, and Googling, and they're not about to stop once they've hit the working world.

Nor should they. Those skills are big assets when it comes to multitasking and productivity. But they're also a nightmare for many of their over-35 bosses, who understand that while technology is a useful tool, it doesn't replace in-person interaction as a primary means of doing business. Today's bosses, like Jerry McGruder, can't understand why their young employees, for all their brains and technical acumen, hardly ever walk in the door, sit down, and actually talk to them. The Generation Y employees often use instant messaging (IM), rather than talking to someone in person—frequently sending messages without thinking. What some Gen Y'ers don't see is that the meaning and value of gestures and other nonverbal skills don't come through in a text message.

Many organizations are finding that they need to emphasize face-to-face and telephone skills, which they see as lacking in IM-happy college grads. The good news is that most new hires are smart, talented, and open to learning. Where they differ from their predecessors is in their requests for more hands-on, interactive training. However, you may find that some do not have the patience to sit through an eight-hour class. You have to talk fast to keep their attention.

Is it possible that it's the older workers who will ultimately have to adjust, forced to do away with the personal touch in favor of pure speed and efficiency? After all, the young tech-savvy employees of today are tomorrow's company bosses. The answer is yes—and no. While increasingly faster communications are here to stay, face-to-face skills have been a staple for getting business done for too long to think they will ever go out of style altogether. There will likely be a happy medium. If you can't build relationships with people, you can't do business.

WORKING OUT THE GEN GAP

With all these differences, is it any wonder that the generations can piss each other off? What is the solution? Ideally, the generations should try to learn from each other. Try to pair young workers with older ones. The young may be able to help the older with technology; the older can teach social and business etiquette skills. One of my clients, a pharmaceutical company, did just that. Getting ready for a merger, they found the younger research and development scientists in a tizzy because they had never worked for anything other than a start-up organization. They were being acquired by a large pharmaceutical giant. The solution: Pair them with old hands who had been through more mergers and spinoffs than could be counted. The surprising perk was that the older workers became more technologically savvy and learned some new research techniques—not to mention picking up some tips on downloading oldies to their iPods!

Clueless Behavior versus Actionable Behavior

While 24/7 communication can be a boon for productivity, it also creates environments ripe for inappropriate communication and its ensuing conflict. "The most important thing, whether it's e-mail or instant messaging, is that the technology gives you a chance to communicate before you think," says Rita Kirk, professor of communications at Southern Methodist University. Consider the extreme case of former Florida Congressman Mark Foley, who became the poster boy for bad judgment when his sexually explicit text communications with teenage congressional pages led to his abrupt resignation.

As outlined in Chapter 3, behavior crosses the line when it's threatening, sexual, and racial or based on some other protected characteristic. For some reason, however, people continue to think that e-mail at work is private; it's not. The company owns its own mail system and has a right to access it at any time. With regard to your own behavior, assume that your boss or a judge is reading your e-mail. Remember: the "e" in "e-mail" stands for evidence.

If someone is e-mailing, instant messaging, or text messaging you inappropriately, you need to ask that person to stop, using one of the techniques described in the next chapter, or complain to HR or your manager using one of the techniques discussed in Chapter 16, if the skills in the next chapter fail. As a general rule, it's always best to first try to talk to the person directly before going to your manager or HR.

He Said/She Said: Ending the War of the Sexes

In her new memoir, *Tough Choices*, Carly Fiorina, the expelled CEO of Hewlett-Packard—and the first female head of a *Fortune* 20 company—explains that she prided herself at succeeding in a man's world without whining about sexism. On her first day at HP, she proclaimed, "The glass ceiling doesn't exist." Now? Not so much . . .

"I think somehow men understand other men's need for respect differently than they understand it for a woman," Fiorina told Lesley Stahl on *60 Minutes*. The male-dominated board's handling of her exit was "heartless in some ways and disrespectful in other ways," she said. "Maybe they took great pleasure in seeing me beat up publicly for weeks and weeks.

"In the chat rooms around Silicon Valley, from the time I arrived until long after I left HP, I was routinely referred to as either a 'bimbo' or a 'bitch,'" she writes. "Too soft or too hard, and presumptuous, besides." She adds, "I watched with interest as male CEOs fired people and were hailed as 'decisive.' I was labeled 'vindictive.'" She reels off things that offended her: The editor of *BusinessWeek* asked her if she was wearing an Armani suit. She felt that adjectives such as "flash," "glamorous," and "diamond-studded" were meant to make her seem superficial. Rarely, she argues, are male executives' styles examined in such depth.

Stories referred to her by her first name. There was "painful commentary" that she'd chosen not to have children because she was "too ambitious." (Even though, Fiorina actually had two children.) "When I finally reached the top, after striving my entire career to be judged by results and accomplishments," she concludes, "the coverage of my gender, my appearance, and the perceptions of my personality would vastly outweigh anything else."

The latest entrant into the gender wars, Columbia Business School, has introduced a new program that teaches the importance of a more empathetic and sensitive leadership style in global business. Students learn how to read facial expressions, body language, and posture, and get coaching on their brain's "mirror neurons"—how what they're thinking and feeling can affect others. "This less autocratic leadership style draws on capabilities in which women are as good as men," says Michael Morris, a professor of psychology and management, who is running the business school's new program.

Daniel Goleman, whose new book *Social Intelligence* is being taught in the program, points out that "while women are, in general, better at reading emotions, men tend to be better at managing them during crises. Women tend to be more sophisticated in reading social interactions but also tend to ruminate more when things go wrong."

While some might quibble with this broad statement, you, as a worker, may need to strengthen your own communication skills in order to deal skillfully with the opposite sex. Again, it's not a matter of right or wrong but of changing the one person we do have control over: ourselves. We can learn how to be flexible with our own communication styles.

One of my clients learned the hard way that the war of the sexes still rages in the workplace. Coached by a mentor at her old law firm to be direct with support staff, she endeavored to do that at a new firm. She was brief, clear, and direct. It failed miserably. Although the terms *law firm* and *soft culture* often don't belong in the same sentence, my coaching client didn't recognize that the new firm did, indeed, have a much softer culture. Consequently, the support staff found her approach to be nothing more than condescending and abrupt antics.

She—as did Fiorina—had run smack into the old gender stereotype: men can be rewarded for hard-charging and direct, even angry behavior, but women may be penalized for the same tactics. Instead of being applauded, they're called bitches. I had to inform my client of the sad truth that women's styles are still examined differently. Women who fail in male-dominated workplaces leave a trail behind them: "We tried hiring a woman but it didn't work out." You rarely hear, "We tried hiring a man but it didn't work out." It's not fair; it's not legal; but it does still happen.

My colleague Rita Risser tells the story of the time she was brought into a well-known Silicon Valley company by the CEO, who wanted to fire the highest-ranking and only woman on his executive team. "Why do you want to fire her?" she asked.

"Because she gets emotional in staff meetings."

"What do you mean, emotional? Does she sob and disrupt the meeting?"

"No, she just sits there and little tears come down, but I feel manipulated."

"Well, is anyone else being emotional in staff meetings?"

He said no, but the HR director, who happened to be a woman, said yes, "Joe Schmoe—he gets emotional."

"What does he do?" asked Rita.

"He screams and yells and when he really gets upset, he throws his shoe across the room."

Rita advised the CEO that if he was going to fire the woman on his senior team for "being emotional," he also needed to fire Joe for "being emotional."

Despite the historic numbers of women in the workplace, these kinds of gender stereotypes persist, creating epic battles.

The key is to try to avoid stereotypes, yet acknowledge differences. It's a tricky paradox.

Recognize that some clashes *may* be the result of differences in gender communication styles, but do not assume or stereotype someone because of his or her gender. Because gender differences may sometimes show up as cultural differences, it can be helpful to try the technique outlined in the next section for communicating effectively with someone from a different culture.

There are many other diversity clashes in the workplace these days: ethnic, racial, sexual orientation, language, to name a few more. There is so much latent power in diversity. If you can learn to respect the diversity of your talent pool and bring together the unique gems that each person offers, your team and your company will profit.

How to Keep Differences from Turning into Difficulties

Coco Chanel captured an enduring truth in one sentence: "In order to be irreplaceable one must always be different." Louis D. Brandeis, the first Jewish Associate Justice on the United States Supreme Court, also captured the importance of uniqueness when he said, "America has believed that in differentiation, not in uniformity, lies the path of progress. It acted on this belief; it has advanced human happiness, and it has prospered."

If differences make us a better nation, a more relevant organization, a more innovative and successful company, we're going to have to learn to cope with differences while also putting them to good use. Of course people are going to disagree! Sometimes people are going to misunderstand each other. They're going to have values and priorities that are so intense, there's spontaneous combustion when they collide. Welcome

STOP Pissing Me Off!

to the real world. The key is to figure out how to deal with the differences and maximize every individual best practice.

Sometimes a festering conflict with a coworker is actually a clash of cultures, fueled by sex, race, or generational differences. We need to realize that as varied as cultures are, so too are their approaches to conflict and communications. Although diverse work groups produce more creative results, they also require more sophisticated communication skills as well as training. Working successfully with people who are very different from you requires skill.

If you're trying to creatively manage a conflict with someone who pisses you off, you need to recognize when it's actually a cultural clash; otherwise, communication will stall.

For example, the dominant culture in this country values a conflict resolution model that is rather confrontational. As a culture, we see ourselves like twenty-first-century John Waynes. This is especially true in organizations where there is a male-dominant culture. We talk straight and we shoot straight. Yet this model is different from that used in many cultures, in which direct confrontation is considered rude. Instead, those cultures value the use of mediators. Conflict management is accomplished through a third party—a trusted family friend, a priest, or an adviser.

One way to find out if a conflict is culture-related is to ask the following questions:

- Have attempts at creatively managing this conflict failed?
- Is the present conflict one of a series?
- Does the conflict seem emotional beyond what you would predict based upon the immediate problem?
- Are the people involved in the conflict from different cultures? Are there obvious differences in race, gender, education, age, or work groups?

If you determine you have a clash of cultures, try the following:

- Gain Agreement: Work with those involved to help them understand:
  - *There is a conflict.*
  - *We share a common goal to creatively manage it.*
  - *What we've tried so far hasn't worked.*

- Identify Hot Buttons
  - Say something like, *"There seems to be something that 'X' says, or that I say, that always sets you off. What is it?"*
  - Clarify back to the person: *"It seems that what sets you off is . . ."*

- Look for a Cultural Source
  - *Ask something like, "Is this an important concern for you?"*

Caution: Do not say, "With your background as an African American (or woman, Generation X'er, and so on.), is this an important concern?" There are many different aspects of our background that create our culture. Allow the coworker (if he or she chooses) to bring up exactly what factors in his or her background drive the reaction.

If You Really Loved Me You Would

It's sort of a no-brainer that good communication is essential to working with people who are different and in dealing with people who piss us off. As the workplace becomes more diverse, good communication is even more important. What we miss, however, is an understanding that our perception about the amount of power we hold in any interaction influences our communication style. This is a critical point; the amount of power you think you have influences how you communicate.

RAPPORT VERSUS REPORT TALK

Linguists tell us that if we perceive we have less power than the person or group that we're communicating with, we will engage in what linguist Deborah Tannen calls "rapport talk." This is talk designed to improve and build relationships. It is conciliatory, polite, and friendly. When using rapport talk, we say things such as, "You might be unaware that . . ." before delivering a nasty blow. We may also say things such as, "I'm not sure if this is right, but maybe we should . . ." We ask permission before we do things: "Would you mind if I . . . ?" We tend to ask for the other person's advice and approval.

If we believe that we have more or equal power with the person we're talking to, we tend to use what Tannen calls "report talk." This is communication that focuses on delivering information and accomplishing tasks. This talk tends to sound like orders. When we use this talk we tend to start our sentences with "I (or we) need to do X." "I want or need X."

In her book *You Just Don't Understand*, Tannen suggests that women tend to use more rapport talk, while men favor report talk. Some linguists agree with Tannen, while others point to the difference in power as the key differentiator. Because women have tended to have less power in most workplaces, they tend to use rapport talk. Studies have found that other groups that historically have had less power, such as African Americans, also use rapport talk. Significantly, people may use one kind of talk in the workplace and another kind of talk at home, where they believe they have a different amount of power.

This difference in the use of rapport talk or report talk also applies to groups in the workplace. Teams can tend to use one style or another, based on perceived power. Groups that tend to use report talk may view other groups as weak, ineffectual, or wasting time because they use so much rapport talk. Conversely, the group that tends to use communication to develop rapport may view the group that uses report talk as brusque, cold, angry, or rude. Members of either group are likely to be frustrated with the other, and this can cause escalating tensions between teams, departments, or divisions. Countless conflicts result from this difference of perception.

It's worthwhile to examine this more closely. Ask yourself the following questions:

- Which of the two styles do you find yourself using at work?
- With whom do you use a different style?
- What is the primary style used by the people in power at work?
- What would the benefits be to you of using a different style?
- What benefits to the organization would there be if you used different styles, as appropriate, for different situations?
- Is your style the one most likely to create what you want at work?

There is no right or wrong style in all situations. The key to managing diversity issues with people who piss you off is to stop and think before you speak (or IM!) in order to determine which communication style is most appropriate in any given situation. In addition, listening carefully will also help you slow down and welcome the opinions of others—especially those who piss us off!

While some of you may wonder whether organizations will ever learn to take advantage of the rich mosaic of today's work force, we can look to the many smart companies that have learned to harness the power of differences. The wildly successful Chipotle Mexican Grill, for example, engages a diverse cast of workers by paying Spanish speakers to learn English and English speakers to learn Spanish. Their teams sling their fresh, tasty, burritos made only from the meat of free-range animals with a camaraderie that's palpable as soon as you enter their restaurants. The company is one of the stock market's darlings while paying its workers way above average for the industry. It also has one of the lowest turnover rates in the fast-food business.

Here are some concrete ways that you can improve communication with people who are different from you:

1. Get to know new people. Reveal a bit about your background. Invite, but do not insist, that they share theirs.
2. Be honest. Reveal that you are trying to improve your own communication style. Ask for suggestions. Ask what kind of communication works for them.
3. Learn about other cultures. Be open to learning about differences. There are many resources in Appendix A of this book to help.
4. Apologize if you think you've offended someone. Ask what you could do differently next time.

Why Do They Do That?

That's the ultimate question, isn't it? Why do people do things that piss us off, annoy us, and leave us frothing at the mouth? Are they just doing it to annoy us? Are they oblivious to how they come across to others? Couldn't they stop if they really wanted to?

My own view is that people are hardwired with certain personality characteristics, some of which can be extremely annoying. The brain is genetically loaded to a certain extent (psychologists currently estimate at least 50 percent) to be focused or distracted, gregarious or withdrawn, good at reading social cues or terrible. While good or bad parenting, cultural influences, education, spiritual work, and therapy can change and influence this, we all arrive on the planet with certain inherent tendencies, strengths, and weaknesses. Understanding how other people's brains might be hardwired can help us cope with their seemingly bizarre (to us) behavior.

You may be surprised to be learning so much about serious mental health issues in a book about working with difficult people. Here's the reason: In my consulting practice, when I'm called in to mediate a group conflict, coach a problem executive, or rebuild a team, I uncover one of these issues at least 80 percent of the time.

Mental Health Problems at Work

Let me give you a couple of examples. One involved a claim of sexual discrimination by the female employees in the legal department of a high-tech company. They believed that they were being treated differently than were the men in the department, who were allowed to work flexible hours and were held to different (lower) standards of productivity.

The main example of the different treatment was an attorney I'll call Bob. When I dug under the surface, it turned out that while working at the office late at night, Bob terrified one of the women ("Mary") by having a complete breakdown:

throwing things, screaming, talking about suicide. She was understandably terrified. She left the office and complained to the company's general counsel the next day.

Mary knew that Bob had been given time off to recuperate, a decision with which she agreed; clearly he needed a time-out! Yet when he returned to work, he was also allowed a flexible schedule and permitted to work at home even though Mary, who had a new baby, had been denied such perks. Also, she and other women attorneys believed that Bob was not held to the same high performance standards that they were. To top it off, they all chorused in when I interviewed them, he was a lousy attorney.

Discrimination, they claimed.

My investigation revealed that they *were* being treated differently, but not because of sex. Bob had been diagnosed as bipolar and his doctor had suggested the reduced and work-at-home schedule.

Medical matters and accommodations for mental disabilities such as this must be kept confidential by the employer, so no one could tell the women why Bob was being allowed the flexible schedule. I found no discrimination in this case, even though I did recommend to the general counsel that even with accommodation for disabilities, he needed to make sure Bob was meeting performance standards. The women, of course, were disappointed in my finding, and I regretted that I could not reveal the underlying issue. Unfortunately, examples such as this are incredibly common.

Another situation I mediated involved a large trade association. The head meeting planner was labeled as "difficult" by many of her coworkers. She'd worked for an authoritarian, structured government agency before being hired by the trade association, which had a relaxed style. Clashes were common.

Her personality style didn't help: She tended to have poor people skills, failed to develop rapport with her coworkers, and snapped at them when she was under stress. In fact, she yelled so loudly that one woman filed a claim under the organization's policy about threats and violence.

When I investigated, I found that the meeting planner was being treated for hepatitis C with a new experimental drug. I happened to know from another client investigation that such drugs cause mood swings and temper tantrums, even though they are lifesaving.

Theoretically, I should not have advised my client about this potential issue, but I knew the drug was impacting the meeting planner's mood and performance. Yet even if they knew why she acted the way she did, they could not discipline or fire her because of the disability issue.

Last but not least, I was brought in to resolve a discrimination complaint among a group of utility construction workers. When I interviewed these large, tough men, they had no interest in talking about the claim. What they wanted to discuss was "Scotty," a coworker they'd toiled with for years who had undergone a dramatic personality change in the past few months. They were afraid he would "go postal," but none of their supervisors would listen to them.

Scotty's wife had left him, and his oldest son was in jail on drunk-driving charges. Not only that; he revealed, when I talked with him, that his much-beloved dog had just died. Talk about a plot for a bad country song!

It turned out that the executive vice president would not listen to me either when I counseled him that he should have a medical evaluation done for Scotty. I had to pull in the outside counsel to convince the EVP, and even then the EVP agreed to the exam grudgingly, since he himself had worked his way up through the ranks to his current position, knew "Scotty," and found him harmless.

A psychologist who specializes in threat evaluations found that Scotty was indeed dangerously depressed, potentially prone to violence, and "unfit for duty." He was placed on medical leave.

I've mediated many such cases in my years as an employment attorney. Often, they don't have easy resolutions—for the "difficult" employee or the colleagues and managers who have to deal with him. However, understanding and compassion do help. Consider the fact that the difficult person in your work group may not be just difficult, but very ill.

The Structure of Brain-Based Illness

Part of the problem we have is that we're hovering on the cutting edge of a virtual revolution in brain science. Neurologists have learned more about the brain in the past ten years than in the previous hundred! Yet, most of us are still stuck in a time warp. We live in a culture that largely believes that behavior is a matter of choice and/or good therapy. However, thanks to the latest research in brain science, there is increasing acknowledgment in the scientific community that some people are just born with personalities that are challenging to the norm.

What an increasing number of neuropsychologists and psychiatrists will tell you is that in effect, people really are hardwired, and that hardwiring will not be tamed or controlled by any software we might use. To a certain extent, people really can't help being the way they are.

This doesn't mean that you should put up with abuse or incompetence in the workplace. However, you need to realize that most of what we think of as annoying is not likely to change, nor is it the result of any particular individual resisting change.

So, to at least some extent, our task is to (1) increase our *understanding* of why people are they way they are, (2) decrease our own stress level so we're not so reactive to others' flaws, and (3) increase our tolerance of others' differences and annoying eccentricities.

Repeat this mantra often: I can't change what I can't change!

No Brain, No Gain: Knowledge Is Power

We live in an exciting and wonderful time for understanding how the brain works and how it affects mood and attention. My own experience is that many of the things our coworkers do that we can't stand are caused by either mood or attention problems. In addition, our own reactivity to these problems may also be caused by our own mood or attention problems. While there are many excellent resources for learning more about this in Appendix A of this book, I will present a vastly oversimplified version of these issues here.

A simple way of thinking about the brain is that it is roughly divided into thirds in terms of function. The feeling part of the brain, or limbic system, is the seat of emotional balance, mood relationship, intimacy, spiritual connection, and all the pleasure drives (or overdrives). The thinking part of the brain, the pre-frontal cortex, is the seat of knowledge, insight, planning, and decision-making, while the brain stem or reptilian brain orchestrates bodily processes.

Neuropsychologists have referred to the pre-frontal cortex of the brain as being akin to a conductor of an orchestra. It is also referred to as "executive function." People who have attention and focus problems are said to have executive function problems. These people could possibly have Attention Deficit Disorders (ADD), although many other things can also affect executive function. Many people who may not meet the clinical definition for ADD do have executive function problems, or low levels of executive function.

"Attention problems" or "attention issues" seem like benign terms, and yet such problems can affect every bit of a person's life. Consider the conductor analogy. A person can have an IQ that is off the charts, a sunny, giving personality, and great musical gifts, but even with these individual superstar performers in the brain, the person will have many challenges if there is no conductor. Imagine, if you will, the Philadelphia Orchestra with Jean-Pierre Rampal as the flutist, the rock-star violinist from the Trans-Siberian Orchestra as the first chair violinist, and a kindergartener conducting. Imagine the chaos!

In the workplace, these people with "attention differences" can sometimes be brilliant, witty, and charismatic, but you may become frustrated by the fact that sometimes, they appear unable to stay on task.

Even if you are open-minded, compassionate, and bend over backward to educate yourself about your colleagues' emotional problems or imbalances, it may not be possible to tolerate having them in the workplace. You may need to skillfully confront them about their behavior, complain to HR, and/or fire them if you're their manager. Before deciding which action to take, it helps to understand why their behavior may be occurring. Sometimes, the reason someone bothers us so much is because we think that they're purposely behaving the way they are. If we can depersonalize this issue, we can calm down and plan our best options.

If their disorganization, problems with attention or impulse control, or hyperfocus on the wrong things causes problems for your business or makes it impossible for you to do your job, something needs to happen. However, it's not helpful to become an armchair doctor and attempt to diagnose medical problems without an appropriate clinical background. Let the qualified medical professionals provide the diagnosis and recommend treatment. Even if you think you're sure about a diagnosis, keep your opinions to yourself and your non-work confidants. Certain kinds of mental disabilities may be legally protected in the workplace and if you spout off about them, you could be subjected to defamation or discrimination claims. Further, unless you're a doctor, there is no way to be sure of someone's diagnosis.

What you can offer, however, is compassion and understanding. Both will go a long way toward helping you work with such people successfully. In the right job, with the appropriate structure and support (and/or the right medication) these people can be brilliant, creative, and successful.

In The Mood: Understanding Clinical Depression

Have you ever worked with someone who was like Eeyore in *Winnie-the-Pooh*—dour, negative, and depressed, even on the sunniest days? This person may be dealing with chronic and clinical depression. Those dark moods can affect others in the workplace. Modern brain science is validating what many of us know instinctively: Depression is catching.

One reason this is so is because of what neuropsychologists call limbic brain resonance. The limbic part of our brain is the portion that governs mood and feeling. Again, we may be genetically loaded to be happy or sad, optimistic or hopeless. We can work to change these things (and if you want to try, Martin Seligman's book *Learned Optimism* is a great place to start), but if we have clinical depression working against us, either genetic or brought on by trauma, it can be an uphill, frequently impossible challenge.

Our limbic brains are, to some extent, wired to resonate in concert with others. When you work with someone who is suffering from untreated clinical depression, his or her brain can affect yours in ways that you may not consciously imagine.

This is because, as explained in Chapter 4, we're wired to connect. New brain imaging technology shows that when we see, hear, or feel someone else's emotions, our brains light up in the same areas as those of the person we're with. The neural pathways in the feeling part of our brains fire the same as if we were experiencing the feeling ourselves. Some people, of course, are even more sensitive to this kind of "emotional contagion," but most of us experience it to some extent. You will need to work hard to protect yourself from catching another person's mood.

Unfortunately, today "only 20 percent of people with major depression get even minimally adequate treatment, and 43 percent aren't being treated at all," says Dr. Thomas Insel, director of the National Institute of Mental Health (*www. nimh.nih.gov*). The costs are staggering: Mental illness causes more disability cases than any other form of illness in adults in America and accounts for well more than $100 billion in lost productivity each year. Sufferers also have a higher risk of developing illnesses such as heart disease, and an increased risk of substance abuse and suicide. Dr. Insel notes that while the United States has about 18,000 homicides a year, it has more than 31,000 suicides.

In any year, nearly 10 percent of the U.S. population suffers from depression. In my experience, depressives cause workplace disruptions far beyond the statistics.

WHAT YOU CAN DO

What do you do about this dilemma? First of all, recognize the symptoms of clinical depression: negativity, irritation, unreasonable outbursts, sadness, and sleep problems. Have compassion for the person who may be suffering from these problems. The Shirley MacLaine character in *Steel Magnolias* nailed depression perfectly when she said, "I'm not crazy, I've just been in a very bad mood for the last forty years!" If you know such a person well, as a friend, it may be appropriate to gently and carefully suggest that he or she seek medical attention. However, you should think this through and be very cautious in doing so.

You especially need to be careful about talking to the person if you're his or her supervisor. Employees have a right to keep their medical problems private. If you don't know for sure that someone is being treated, speaking about it is even more problematic. You especially want to avoid talking about your suspicions to others because that could constitute defamation. At the least, it could be a privacy violation.

If you suspect that someone is suffering from an untreated mental illness, your best course is to offer some version of the following: "If there's anything going on at work that's affecting your success, please let me know. If there's anything going on in your personal life that's affecting your success, that's none of my business, but we have employee assistance that you could contact."

Thus, you open that door but you do not walk through it. If the person volunteers something about his or her condition, you can be compassionate but should avoid giving advice. It is okay to share your own experience if you've dealt with a similar situation.

Bipolar Illness in the Workplace

People who have bipolar disorder (which used to be called manic-depression) can wreak havoc in any workplace. While experts estimate that only 2 to 3 percent of Americans suffer from this disorder, those who do can have a large impact. Typically, these people can be up, down, or sideways on any given day. They also can run on nothing but air for days and weeks, accomplishing an incredible amount of brilliant work with no sleep or food, dazzling everyone with their success.

Medical researchers are now realizing that many people who are struggling at work or at home oftentimes have a milder form of bipolar disorder. Untreated, this disease gets much worse. Life is difficult for people who suffer from bipolar disorder. They frequently suffer from sleep problems, especially in the spring and summer, and they may have trouble getting out of bed in the winter. At work, performance may be uneven. It may be great one week, or for a month, or a year, and then their performance may flop for an equal amount of time. For a brilliant and compassionate memoir on this problem, read *Unquiet Mind* by Kay Redfield Jamison. Jamison has suffered from bipolar disorder for years and now serves as a psychiatry professor at Johns Hopkins School of Medicine, where she specializes in the disorder that plagues her.

Bosses and colleagues will shake their heads, mystified about such people. What can we do about this uneven performance? How can this individual do so well and then so terribly? In addition, people with mood problems (whether bipolar or unipolar) will frequently be difficult to motivate with external reinforcement. People who suffer from mood disorders can be extremely sensitive to both criticism and blame, frequently having their antennae up for anything that smacks of defamation of their character. Even positive comments can be taken the wrong way.

WHAT YOU CAN DO

Again, diagnosis by amateurs can be dangerous. Don't try this at home! My experience is, however, that understanding why some people may act in such unpredictable ways can help you calm down your own tendency to blame them and help you strategize more productive interactions. The best way to handle colleagues like this is to focus on making specific requests for them to change their *behavior* (not their attitude, or their personality), as you'll learn in the next chapter. The problem is that they may not be able to change their behavior to line up with your request. At that point you'll need to consider your options: work around them, complain to a higher authority, or move on to another job, which is discussed in later chapters.

Just Checking

There are some micromanagers among us. These are the people who lean-in, butt-in, stick their noses in and generally go where no one has invited them to appear. These people may be suffering from Obsessive Compulsive Disorder (OCD) and/or extreme anxiety disorder. Lesser examples of these personality traits—which may not reach the clinical level—are seen in the micromanagers among us, both the bosses and the colleagues in our workplace who have to have their hands in everything. At the extreme levels, they may check and recheck their own work and everyone else's. They may insist that all details are important and may want you to pay attention to things that don't add value to the bottom-line result.

Again, many matching problems result from this. If you're in the don't-sweat-the-small-stuff camp, you will curse these people as overbearing nervous ninnies. If you never saw a detail that you didn't like, you'll love working with such people. Detail-oriented jobs such as accounting or law may be perfect places for these traits.

If the traits are extreme, however, sufferers may be driven to distraction by their own behavior. Classic examples include returning to the house three times to make sure that the stove is turned off, that the refrigerator door is closed, and the faucet isn't running. At the more extreme end of the spectrum, people suffering from OCD may wash their hands compulsively, scrub floors that are already spotless, and engage in other extreme behaviors. At that level, of course, they need medical intervention.

More mild forms of anxiety and compulsion abound, however, and working with a micromanager can be painful.

Again, once you understand that a person's behavior is meant not to annoy you but to manage his or her own anxiety, you may find that the behavior doesn't bother you as much. If you're still bothered, you can make skillful requests for change in behavior as outlined in the next chapter. Because such people may not be able to change, however, a good tactic is to assign them tasks that are well aligned with their personalities. For example, you could ask them to fact-check your articles. In the right job, all that perfectionism can be a blessing. If that's not possible, you can still complain to HR or leave, as outlined in later chapters.

All Mixed Up

Of course, brain chemistry issues can exist in a variety of forms and combinations. For example, a person can have both a bipolar and attention deficit hyperactivity disorder (ADHD) diagnosis. The leading psychiatrists and neuropsychologists in this arena will tell you that many of these labels are a requirement for treatment and demanded by insurance companies, but that they don't really describe the totality of the person and the individual problem. If you've ever suffered from the flu, had broken ribs, and needed a root canal all in the same week, you can understand how complex it is to have more than one medical issue at one time. On the flip side, not everyone who's difficult has a biological mental disorder. You may also work with people who have what are called *character disorders.*

CHARACTER DISORDERS

"My boss is a psychopath," a client of mine insists. "She is a pathological liar!" Psychopaths, sociopaths, borderline, and schizoid personalities are what are called character disorders. Generally (although there is some dispute about this among experts), these are parts of our characters that are formed by our life experiences rather than by our genetic makeup. Abuse, neglect, or trauma can each lead to character disorders. Of course, these character defects can be fueled or even driven by the various brain chemistry problems described in the previous sections.

You can imagine how hard it would be to work with someone who lies pathologically, without remorse; who hurts people without caring; who is prone to violence or who has a cruel streak. If a person like this is in an authority position over you, you are in a very difficult tight spot with only limited options. Voice your concerns diplomatically to your supervisor's boss and/or to your HR director. If the situation doesn't change, quietly hunt for another job and get out of there as fast as you can (see Chapter 16 for more about both of these options). There truly is no winning if you're working for one of these people. Be careful, however, about making this diagnosis. Work your way through understanding and compassion first, and then consider the paradigm you're using—in other words, from what point of view and context are you viewing the situation?

I hope that, a result of reading this chapter, you've begun to stop taking other people's behavior personally. Perhaps they're acting the way they are because of cultural, gender, or generational differences; perchance they're suffering from brain-based biological illness or character disorders. No matter. Instead of fretting about *why* they're doing what they're doing or whether they're doing it just to piss you off, you, now enlightened, will concentrate your energies on learning how to respond skillfully, which is the subject of the next few chapters. You'll stop wasting your energy yelling at their boat for ramming you, and instead learn how to navigate your own craft with speed and style.

YOUR RELATIONSHIP TOOLBOX

HOW TO MOVE FROM PISSED OFF TO POWERFUL	
PISSED OFF	POWERFUL
Wasting time wondering why	Quickly understand why, then move on
Wishing people were more like you	Valuing differences among people
Assume someone could change if they wanted to	Realize most people can't change who they are
Asking someone to change their nature	Skillfully requesting behavior changes

06.
HAVE I TOLD YOU LATELY THAT
YOU BUG ME?

How to have difficult conversations with
difficult people.

Sue is pissed! Her coworker in the next cube clears his throat
every ten to twelve seconds, every single work day, without fail.
The noise is so loud that callers on her line ask if she is in the
car with the motor running. Not one to suffer in silence, Sue
has made her feelings known—to her sister, her mother, her
girlfriends, even the bartender at her neighborhood pub. Occasionally, she yells "Be quiet!" over the walls in the general direction of the guy who's driving her insane, but nothing changes.
At this rate, she's going to have to wear earmuffs to work.

Learn the Art of Winning, Not Whining

Why do we whine? Do we really think that it gets results?
Psychologist Gay Hendricks believes that when the whining
involves another person, we're criticizing that person because
we believe that regardless of whether we've asked someone
to do (or not do) something, there was an implied agreement
that was broken—for example, not making a noisy nuisance of

yourself. There is another truth as well, and that is that most of us haven't learned how to make effective requests in the first place. Instead, we complain.

Consider this common workplace scenario: A team leader wants someone on his team to develop a better attitude, and so has a number of conversations with the employee about the employee's bad attitude. However, nothing changes. The bad attitude still oozes everywhere. The team leader keeps talking; the employee keeps resisting. No surprise, really. Why? Because the leader has failed to explain exactly what behavior he does want. Instead, he just keeps complaining about the employee's *attitude*, a vague term that could mean anything.

Isabella, for example, is a bright young director of a high-tech company. The company requested coaching from me after she had several run-ins with lower-level staff people who complained constantly about her condescending, harsh attitude. Talks with HR failed to change her behavior. The tech company really wanted to retain Isabella, because she was brilliant at her work. They also feared they'd be slapped with a lawsuit if they canned her. When I met with the senior leaders of the organization, they summed up the problem in the same manner as did the subordinates: Isabella was harsh and condescending in her tone. I listened to numerous examples of "he said/she said."

Frustrated, I requested the performance reviews. They were similarly vague and unhelpful. Moreover, they were so loosely done that it's likely they'd never stand up to legal scrutiny, despite the fact that they had allegedly been reviewed by the firm's employment attorneys. The reviews were laced with subjective comments, including that her attitude was "condescending," "brusque," and "short with staff."

The problem resides with the word *attitude*: It can have different connotations depending upon context. If you're a punk rocker or a rap singer, attitude is everything. Labeling someone with attitude can be a compliment. However, when it comes to performance, the word is anemic. It generates confusion, caution, and a whole lot of nothing. It's not attitude you're after. It's behavior. My client needed to learn how to make specific, behavioral requests, and so do you.

A MATTER OF APPROACH

In the workplace, you've got lions and tyrants and boors who will only respond to behavioral requests. Instead of asking them to change an attitude, you must make it a measurable, objective, observable behavior for which the person is held accountable. Consider Isabella. Instead of talking about being harsh or condescending, I coached her to change the way she interacted. I gave her tools regarding what to say and do. In place of Isabella's usual approach of dropping a project on a subordinate's desk and barking orders, I coached her to hand off that project differently. She learned to introduce the issue softly, saying something such as "Do you have a minute to talk about a new project? Is this a good time to talk?" "What's your work load; do you have time to take on new work?"

FOCUS ON THE BEHAVIOR

The key is to forget about attitude and deal with behavior. You'll find that's actually easier because it's clear and straightforward as opposed to vague and subjective. If you are judging someone's work ethic, level of engagement, or attitude negatively, there are concrete, observable behaviors that are leading you to that conclusion. Spell out the expectations clearly—whatever the issue. Tell a chronically late employee that she has to come in on time. Demand that a person who is frequently having a good time on the phone to eliminate personal phone calls. Ask the Internet shopper to refrain from surfing. You get the idea. It's simple. It's direct. It's unequivocally clear.

Every time you even think about complaining, pause and convert that whining into a specific request. What makes a request specific is that it is actionable. It is something the person can say or do. Anything else is too vague, not measurable, and is unlikely to get the results you need. Whining does nothing except weaken your own mood and the moods of those to whom you speak. Even more important, whining doesn't work.

Requests that Get Results

If you want to deal with any issue that has the potential to be emotionally charged, and you want to get results, try an approach that I call 1-2-3 Go! Here's how it works:

1. Say something to the person that implies understanding or appreciation.
2. Make a behaviorally specific (doable) request. (It has to be something the person can do or say, or it's not behaviorally specific.)
3. Add more appreciation and understanding.
4. Go away; do not nag, hover, or whine.

Let's go back to Isabella. There were several behaviors she needed to change, making it a more complex series of requests.

One request might be:

1. "I know how busy you are, but I need you to soften your requests to staff members. We appreciate how much work you manage to get done around here! You're one of our most productive directors." **(appreciation and understanding)**
2. "Before you ask staff to do something, would you please take the time to ask if they're busy, and if they have time to take on an extra project?" **(doable request)**
3. "I know that this may seem like a picky thing to you, but, trust me; it will make a world of difference to our busy programmers." **(understanding)** "Thank you." **(appreciation)**
4. Go away; do not hover or nag.

Of course, making these kinds of requests requires you to figure out what you want, something many of us dither about. You may know that someone bugs you, or that when you are around the other person, it's like oil and water, but you can't put your finger on what it is. Thus, you need to ponder and reflect on what it is and what reasonable change that person could make. Complete personality transplants are not an option! You have to sort through behavioral, performance-impacting changes that can be made and personality differences that you may need to understand and accept. Simply being annoyed by someone else's personality is not a sufficient reason for that person to have to make a change. Issues that affect your ability to perform, or your team's ability to meet their goals, are worth examining. Reread Chapter 3 if you're still confused about this.

Again, focus on the specific behavior you want to change. It has to be something that the person could say or do that would actually make a difference in the outcome of your performance or the performance of your team or organization. If nothing that they say or do would actually make a difference in your own or team performance, then you need to stop and examine your motives and expectations.

You need to understand why a person drives you crazy. Is it something that "triggers" you? A trigger reminds you of someone or something in the past that was problematic, traumatic, or associated with unpleasantness. If for example, you were constantly criticized as a child and then overcompensated for that criticism by becoming a perfectionist, any workplace criticism may "trigger" painful memories that cause you to overreact.

A trigger may also be something that reminds you of your own shadow side. If you're constantly trying to hide or repress your own temper, you may avoid or clash with someone else who has a bad temper. We all have a darker side of our personality that we try to repress or deny. It's important that you don't impose your own triggers or shadow side on your coworkers. You have no right to darken the doorsteps of colleagues with our own issues. If you're struggling with such an issue, take action. Seek out a trusted adviser; access the confidential employee assistance program at your work, if it's offered. Use a journal, see a therapist, talk to your doctor, seek out a spiritual adviser, or get other assistance.

If you have decided that the issue that's bugging you is affecting performance—yours or others—and that there is something the offending party could say or do differently, craft a specific request. Before you make the request, try role-playing with someone you trust. Then make the request. Walk away and give the person the opportunity and some time to make the change. If the behavior doesn't change, return and repeat the request. If that still doesn't work, repeat one more time before you raise the stakes and step up the action.

Here are some examples of vague requests and specific behavioral-based changes:

VAGUE	SPECIFIC
Stop bothering me!	I can't work when you stand by my desk and talk. Please stop.
Don't be rude to customers.	Greet each customer when he or she arrives. Ask how you can help the customer.
Don't harass the women.	Please don't make comments about your colleagues' appearance.

Consequences that Command Attention

Once you've repeated the request a total of three times, you can shift to a higher gear. This involves adding consequences to your request. For instance, suppose you've asked your coworker three times to stop using his speakerphone because it disturbs your work. Yet he still is doing the same @#$% thing! Add a consequence to the sequence. The next request would look like this:

1. "I know how much you like to use your speakerphone, and I appreciate that sometimes you remember not to do that when I'm working. I understand how hard it can be to change a habit." **(appreciation or understanding)**
2. "I need you to remember not to use it at all when I'm in the office. Please talk on the phone instead." **(specific behavioral request)**
3. "I'm sorry to have to take this step, but if it happens again, I'm going to have to talk to our manager about this. I simply can't get my work done when you do this." **(add consequence)**

4. "Thank you. Again, I know how hard it can be to change and I appreciate your taking these steps for me." **(appreciation and understanding)**
5. Go! Walk away; do not nag, complain, or whine.

Then, of course, if your colleague keeps using the speakerphone, you will need to follow through. The biggest mistake in this process is to delineate consequences and then not pull the trigger. It turns a consequence into an empty threat. When you implement the consequence and talk to the manager, use the same 1-2-3-Go! format. It's your problem, and you need to find a way to deal with it. A conversation with the manager might go like this:

1. "Ms. Manager, I appreciate how busy you are but I really need to talk to you about Steve Speakerphone. Do you have a minute right now?" **(appreciation or understanding)**
2. "I have asked Steve Speakerphone to stop using his speakerphone three times and he keeps doing it. This is affecting my performance. I can't concentrate and, as a result, I'm not hitting my targets. I really need you to talk to him and get him to stop." **(doable request)**
3. "I really appreciate your handling this problem." **(appreciation or understanding)**
4. Listen to any concerns the manager has and then Go! Do not whine, complain, or nag.

Be sure to focus on the impact the person's behavior has on your performance or the performance of your team. Remember, if it's not impacting your performance, the performance of your team, or the organization as a whole, it's not your manager's problem!

What if the manager doesn't respond or doesn't do what you ask? Then you need to repeat your request with her three times. This repetition works best if you don't whine or complain about having to repeat. In fact, start fresh every time with a smile, or at the very least have a pleasant look on your face. If you let your annoyance show, you've undermined your effort. Perhaps your manager has just been too busy to deal with the problem. Perhaps she forgot, or was hoping that the problem would just go away. It never serves you to bring up her lack of focus. People just don't respond well when you point out flaws. It's a sure way to put your manager on the defensive. Graciousness will do the opposite.

IF YOU'RE STILL BEING IGNORED

After three times, and only then, can you ratchet up the consequences. At this point it's a matter of diplomacy. You must analyze your relationship with your manager and ask yourself a crucial question: How important is this issue? Once you determine the importance of the issue, you can decide on one of three options:

- Drop it.
- Go back to your manager and tell her that if she can't or won't deal with it, you need to get her manager or Human Resources involved.
- Go directly to the HR folks and ask them to handle the issue discreetly.

Of course, the problem with this kind of escalation is obvious. Your manager may never forgive you for your end run. One way to protect yourself is to e-mail your thanks to your manager every time you ask for her help, repeating, in that e-mail, what you requested and thanking her in advance for helping you with this problem. This technique serves two purposes: it reminds her and any higher-ups that you did, indeed, do everything possible to try to get her help, and it also gives you a paper trail to back up your belief that you were totally reasonable and professional in trying to solve the problem.

Managing Our Own Emotions

All of this sounds so very reasonable, doesn't it? So why doesn't everyone act this way? For a very simple reason: We don't manage our own emotions. We tend to wait too long to bring up issues and we also often haven't tamed our own minds and hearts. According to psychologists, if we wait too long, we get "flooded" with our emotions and the emotions overtake our minds. We literally lose our minds—at least the part that prompts us to think before we speak. Experts have found that men flood more often than do women, but that it can still affect all of us.

Instead of waiting, it's far more effective to strengthen your own *executive function*, the part of your brain that serves as the orchestra conductor (see Chapter 5) and make sure that you use your executive function instead of the emotional part of your brain.

The nasty truth is that some of us simply do not think before talking. All too often, we try to use talking to figure out what it is we're thinking and feeling. That type of freeform exploration may work in a therapy session—but not in the workplace. You should think *before* talking. When you're dealing with a difficult coworker, you need to take time to cool down before you blow your top.

Blowing off steam with someone removed from the situation may help. Ideally, you should select someone from the outside: a counselor, priest, or even a friend or spouse. Emote, emote, and emote! with your sympathetic listener and get it out of your system. Writing in a journal can also be therapeutic. All of this pre-work will serve you well when you actually sit down with your coworker.

TELL THE TRUTH FAST

Part of the reason many of us blow up so readily is that we wait too long to verbalize our grievances. Develop the habit of bringing up small things that bug you before they become large things. Making tiny, specific, and skillful requests in the 1-2-3-Go! format can manifest great results. If you establish this kind of relationship with your coworkers early on it can help you avoid much pain down the line. My rule: Tell the truth fast; just make sure that you do it as a skillful request, and not a complaint. As mentioned earlier, complaints and whining are 100 percent useless in relationships—whether work related or personal. Use this slogan from now on when you hear yourself complaining or whining: Gee, I could have made a request instead!

If you doubt the concept of telling the truth fast, consider the experience of Ron Suskind, Pulitzer Prize–winning reporter and bestselling author of *The One Percent Doctrine: Deep Inside America's Pursuit of Its Enemies Since 9/11.* He explained that he gets subjects to talk about things they don't want to talk about by telling them to trust the truth. "Truth is what works. It works in your personal life. It works in discussions between citizens and their government, between employees and their bosses. It just does."

AVOID REGRETS!

You are not going to like this rule, I promise you, but it is one of the most important in this cyber-age: When you're dealing with a difficult coworker, you must, must, must meet them in person and never address the issue via e-mail. If you can't make your requests face-to-face, you must pick up the phone and have a real-time conversation—not just leave voice mails. Once relationships tank, e-mailing only escalates the feud.

It's impossible to interpret meaning through e-mail. You miss the facial expressions and emotional tone that provide the all-important context for a discussion. What is context? It's the meaning that you give to the words someone uses. As Lewis Carroll wrote in *Alice in Wonderland*, "When *I* use a word, it means just what I choose it to mean—neither more nor less." We all speak and hear through our own private language. Without the emotions and guidance of someone's face and gestures, we're hopelessly muddled.

In the mediations that I've covered in recent years, at least four of them were called to address conflict caused by e-mailing. One example: A woman filed a harassment complaint against her boss. Her complaint? He did everything using e-mail, all of her assignments, communications, and so on. He even did her performance review by e-mail. The kicker? His office was right next door to hers!

In another situation, a high-tech company hired me to work with a group of developers. This team was so conflicted they couldn't even get the product out the door. They flew me in to observe their weekly staff meeting. The developers all tromped in with their laptops.

This *might* have been useful; perhaps they had the agenda on there or needed to take notes of the meeting. But these clowns constantly e-mailed each other during the meeting with scurrilous e-mail messages. One person would say something aloud in the meeting and three other guys would e-mail things such as, "dog breath, that's the stupidest comment anyone ever made!"

I stared at their screens in disbelief. Why, I wondered, were they paying me so much to understand the obvious problem? Of course, we had to confiscate their laptops and force them to actually talk face-to-face with one another. This proved to be an excruciating exercise for this group but eventually, they improved their communication skills.

Are You Listening To Me?

There may come a time in the whole 1-2-3-Go! process when you must activate that annoying but essential skill of listening. The target of your request may actually want to hold forth on his or her own point of view. If this roadblock occurs, don't be distracted. All the explanations in the world can't stop you from delivering your request! Nod, smile, cluck sympathetically, and repeat your request. If they deliver an absolute knockout "no way," continue to nod, smile, and say, "I understand, but will you do it anyway?" Trust me, if you deliver these responses often enough, they'll decide that they can't get around you and will, in all likelihood, conform to your request just to get rid of you.

If that doesn't work, you really may have to break down and listen. As you do, it can be helpful to consider another of Ron Suskind's tricks for getting people to talk about things they don't want to talk about. "First, make apologies. You say, 'Listen, I'm going to ask you some really stupid questions so bear with me.' But you also say, 'Here's why. . .'" Second, you have to be interested in people, no matter what they do. I'm fascinated by people, and when they see this, they respond. It also helps to consider my 'good enough reasons' rule: People do what they do for good enough reasons. They may not be your reasons or mine, but they're good enough for them. And if they know you're attentive to their motivations, people will tell you the most astonishing things."

LISTEN WELL

Realize that it's hard to listen well—most people don't. Part of the problem is that we live in an increasingly visual world with screens everywhere: computers, video games, TV, and movies. We don't sit around the kitchen table telling stories often enough. We move fast; listening requires that we slow down. We can become passionate in our listening. We can learn to listen with the same energy and enthusiasm that we put into talking. Instead of listening for evidence that confirms our point of view, we can listen for the creative energy in the conflict—both in ourselves and in others. We can listen for what challenges our view in order to understand how others see the world.

When you do decide to listen to find out what the other person's "good enough reason" might be, follow these tips:

1. **Remember filters.** We all hear what is said through our own filters. Filters can include our assumptions, biases, our own history, experience, and so forth.
2. **Listen as a witness.** Ask, "How would I listen to this person if I knew I was going to be called as an objective witness in court?" "How can I listen well enough to hear the still, small voice inside me?"

3. **Clarify.** Before you speak, make sure you understand what the other person is saying. Ask open-ended, non-leading questions (who, what, where, when) until you do understand.

4. **Restate.** Ask, "I think you said 'X'; is that accurate?" Continue restating until your partner agrees that you heard him or her accurately.

5. **Pause before you speak.** Ask yourself which conflict style you're using, and why. Is it the style that will serve you best over the long term of this relationship? Is the response you're considering likely to lead to more satisfaction for you, and more creativity and productivity for your team? What response would be most likely to lead to those results?

6. **At the end of a communication, summarize the conversation and clarify the original reason for the communication.** Did the speaker want your advice, feedback, a sympathetic ear, action, or a solution to a problem? Be sure you know why you were asked to listen and what you're expected to do—if anything—about the communication. Many of us jump in too quickly to give advice or fix a problem before even bothering to ask if the speaker wants advice.

7. **Assume 100 percent of the responsibility for the communication.** Assume leadership in your communication. Assume that it is your responsibility to listen until you understand and to speak in a way others can understand.

8. **Check out misunderstandings.** Assume miscommunication before you assume that someone is trying to undermine your efforts. Effective communication is the exception, not the rule.

Before you end the conversation, make sure that you find out when the other person is going to start doing or saying what you've requested. Also, if the person has repeatedly failed to meet a reasonable agreed-upon request, remind him or her of the agreement and ask straight out, "What's in the way of your meeting this request? It seems that we're both in agreement and that you want to meet the request."

After all this exhausting listening (and it can be tedious), you may decide to change or eliminate your original request. If so, congratulations! You've earned points for flexibility. If not, start over with requests and/or escalate, as described previously. Most of these techniques work well with bosses and customers as well, but in the next few chapters, we'll add some special ideas for these pesky folks. Meanwhile, remember your new mantra: "I could have made a request!"

YOUR RELATIONSHIP TOOLBOX

HOW TO MOVE FROM PISSED OFF TO POWERFUL

PISSED OFF	POWERFUL
Whining and complaining	Making specific requests
Making vague requests	1-2-3-Go! format
Complaining about others' personality characteristics	Focusing only on behavior that impacts performance
Continuing to whine without results	Adding consequences to requests and then escalating if you don't get results
Stuffing feelings until you blow up	Cleaning house; doing emotional housecleaning and making frequent requests
Not listening well	Becoming a good listener

07.
THE BOZO BOSS FROM HELL

How to go around that clown.

Think *your* boss is bad? Consider the character of Miranda Priestly in the bestselling book and movie, *The Devil Wears Prada*. Miranda, editor of *Runway* magazine and grand dame of fashion journalism, devours her assistants like a lion carelessly crunching on baby rabbits. Her latest victim, Andy, has the job millions of girls would kill for—or so she's told time and time again. Miranda treats Andy as yet another fashion accessory: necessary, but clearly her possession. The entire staff walks around on pins and needles trying to accommodate Miranda's insane demands. Not only does she expect her assistants to jump when she asks, but they also must ask, "How high?"

A Paycheck or a Down Payment on Your Soul?

Miranda is a textbook example of the type of bad boss I call the DI (Devils Incarnate). Yet, all bosses who career through the workplace like problem children seem to recite the same mantra when they attempt to corral the troops: "You don't have to like me, but you do have to respect me." The worker bees, already cranky and frothing at the mouth from dealing with this clueless prig, respond silently, or among themselves, with furious indignation.

Who is right here? As usual, no one is totally correct. One of life's painful truths is this: You have to give up certain things in exchange for a paycheck. Among those things is what you might consider the right to disrespect the organization or boss that provides the paycheck. If you don't respect those two entities, you have three choices:

1. Leave.
2. Diplomatically push back (in other words, try to change their way of behaving or appeal to a higher authority to get rid of them).
3. Adjust your own attitude.

Sorry, but staying around and whining is not an acceptable option. Why? For one very pragmatic reason: It does not work. It will make you miserable and eventually it will boomerang back to the boss.

One of my favorite quotes is from Emerson, who said, "Who you are speaks so loudly, I can't hear what you're saying." Unless you're Robert DeNiro or Meryl Streep, you're not going to be able to pull off the illusion that you respect someone when you don't. At some level, they're going to know it and react. Then it will just become a downward spiral that sucks your job and your mental health into the sewer. Is respect earned? Sometimes, but better to respect everyone than to whine ineffectively.

Perhaps you can take solace from the reality that bum bosses are in ample supply. Thanks to the Web, their victims no longer have to suffer in silence; they share loudly and long about their nemeses. Check out Working America's My Bad Boss Contest. This group, affiliated with the AFL-CIO, is collecting anonymous scary workplace stories at its Web site, *www.workingamerica.org/badboss*. Forced overtime, canceled vacations, and reprimands for taking needed sick leave are just the beginning of some bosses' insensitivities.

As discussed in Chapter 3, some boss behavior may be over the legal line, such as when it segues into harassment, discrimination, or even improperly denying leave requests. Clearly, if you're working for this kind of boss you need to file a complaint to HR, your boss's boss or some outside agency, as outlined in Chapter 16, instead of merely whining.

Pick Your Poison—What Flavor Is Your Boss from Hell?

In my experience, bozo bosses come in four types, each one requiring a slightly different strategy:

1. Micromanagers (MMs)
2. Conflict Avoiders (CAs)
3. Clueless Incompetents (CIs)
4. Devils Incarnate (DIs)

In the following sections, I'll help you identify what kind you're dealing with, and give you tips on how to cope.

Micromanagers (MMs)

Micromanagers may or may not suffer from Obsessive Compulsive Disorder (OCD), but they will drive you batty.

My first boss out of law school was an MM. Brilliant but nerdy, he made our office of twenty-plus attorneys sign in and out for lunch and bathroom breaks. Complaints that we were not wage-and-hour slaves and should not be treated as such were dismissed with shrugs. He tore around the office with a pencil behind his ear so he could attack any meandering dangling participles or misplaced modifiers he happened to find sneaking about in our correspondence or briefs. I will admit that he was the best writer I've ever worked with, and we shared a love of modern literature and the hunt for the perfect verb. However, nothing escaped his notice; his relentless pursuit of perfection in the written documents we generated like so many disposable diapers led us to gnash our teeth in frustration.

Jerry (not his real name, all bosses' names have been changed to protect the guilty) had prematurely white hair and the most piercing blue eyes I've ever been stared down by. He hovered around the front door, checking his watch with the dedication of a coach tracking sprinters, so he could readily reprimand those who took bathroom breaks longer than ten minutes. He loped around the office, clucking over his progeny as they labored in order to monitor any hapless workers who mistakenly gazed out the window for more than five seconds.

Yes, Jerry was a nitpicker extraordinaire, but he never understood the power of prioritizing. He perused cover letters for insignificant errors with the same care that he edited a 10th Circuit brief. Because of his obsessions, the big issues were never addressed, such as which projects we focused on and why, and what we accomplished or didn't. I lasted about a year and then bailed. I could not continue to work with someone whose skills seemed so misdirected. Jerry would have served well as a *New York Times* copy editor, but managing a federal agency office tasked with addressing big issues created problems for him and for us.

Perfectionist micromanagers are obsessed with control, convinced that the world will come to an end if certain details are not *peeerfect*. In some jobs, such as surgery, this compulsive attention to the seemingly insignificant is important. However, most bosses need a mix of micro and macro skills, and the wisdom to know when one is best used over another. If you're unlucky enough to be thrown into the forest with someone who can only see the trees, you have my sympathy.

TAMING THE MICROMANAGER

What works with such a boss? Not much. As with most people, they are who they are. Again, it's a matter of matching. If you're also a perfectionist, it's a match made in heaven. If you're more of a big-picture thinker, it may still work if he or she appreciates your talents. Without that appreciation, however, you'll both end up frustrated.

Your best survival strategy with such bosses is surrender: Take their skills and use them to your advantage. Learn everything you possibly can. If your boss is really good at the details of what he or she does, and many MMs are, you can learn a tremendous amount about the details of your job and getting those details right. What you won't gain, however, is perspective—the ability to sort out what's really important from what's not. For that you will eventually have to move on to another boss or organization.

You can try communicating with your MM and, if you're lucky, perhaps reach détente with your boss regarding things that merit relentless supervision and those that do not. With this, however, you'll need to be very specific. It won't work to talk about the problem in general. Try to gain agreement about which projects will be solely in your territory with no supervision and which will not. You will probably have to remind your boss frequently of your agreements, because he or she most likely will forget. The best strategy is to get it in writing—it covers your butt and reassures your boss about what you're doing. Remember, the MM boss needs the illusion of control to feel calm. Without that, he or she will be incredibly nervous and take those nerves out on you.

One of the sad facts of life is that people don't change without enormous incentive to do so. If you try all of these suggestions and he or she is still driving you batty, you can stage a last-ditch effort. Lay your cards on the table and calmly, without blaming or whining, announce that your styles are incompatible and that you will have to leave if things do not change within a specific period. If you're brilliant or valuable enough, your boss may try to accommodate your needs, but be prepared for lots of backsliding while your boss forgets and tries to self-medicate his or her anxiety by controlling you. You may also be able to work around your boss by hiding some projects and working unilaterally. However, these evasive techniques only work in the short run.

Your boss is your boss for one very good reason: The organization thinks (right or wrong) that he or she should be the boss. Whether talent, political skills, organizational incompetence, or sleeping with the boss propelled him or her to the top doesn't matter. You're stuck with your organization's wrongheaded view. You, not they, need to adapt. Remember: Your boss may not always be right, but he or she is always the boss.

Conflict Avoiders (CAs)

When I speak about different conflict styles, my audiences frequently ask me which style causes the most woe in any workplace. Given the more nefarious types of bosses, they're surprised when I single out conflict avoiders.

One of my first consulting projects was with a CEO of a high-tech medical equipment company. Randy was a friendly, polished, experienced corporate games player, who had worked his way up the ranks of a large manufacturing company, and then been tapped for the top job at a company we'll call Med Mechanics. Randy brought me in to work with a conflict in his executive team. Their snapping and snarling at each other had driven him to distraction. Individually, they were a talented and workable lot, but as a group, they bickered incessantly.

After individual interviews with each team player, I surfaced a disturbing question: How could such a nice guy like Randy work with so many snakes?

The answer, of course, was that Randy was the problem. He avoided conflict, ducking decisions and assigning roles in a hazy manner so that no one would be annoyed with him. His executive team expressed the conflicts he habitually avoided.

The solution? I used what I call the "beyond" trick. Groups stuck in habitual conflict frequently fuss and fume about things over which they have no control: assignments, resource constraints, or authority. I had the group sit down and work together (therapeutic in itself) to compile three lists: 1) the conflicts they'd historically harbored, things that no longer were relevant but that they still simmered about; 2) current "hot" issues; 3) "beyond issues": issues they bickered about but over which they had no control. Not surprisingly, the biggest list was the "beyond" issues. I marched into Randy's office with the three lists. "The group worked hard!" I crowed. "But you know, it's the darnedest thing, the biggest list of problems are those over which they have no control. These are all decisions that *you* have to make. I think it's so useful that they identified them for you. Now we can decide what to do about these things."

No dummy, Randy saw the handwriting on the wall and we set to work. Over several similar sessions and my gentle coaching, Randy eventually realized that confront issues he must, or he would suffer the continual mutiny of his troops.

MANAGING A CONFLICT AVOIDER

If you work for a CA, a similar process could be helpful. Gather those most affected by his lack of leadership, come up with the three lists, and present them to him. Again, backsliding will happen, so use this technique whenever unmade decisions pile up and start to smell like unwashed laundry. Of course, if your boss still resists your efforts to gently encourage decision-making, you may need to consider your options of either complaining to a higher authority or seeking another position.

Clueless Incompetents (CIs)

For me, a CI would be the worst kind of boss. I respect talent, and working with the talentless would drag me into a pit of despair. The good news about these bosses is that they may be happy to have you do the work, since they're frequently lazy as well as incompetent. Why is this good news? Because if you love the job or the field you're in, the work itself can be worth it. Moreover, their laissez-faire attitude may enable you to take over projects that could give you valuable experience and contacts. The risk? Don't count on their help if you get in over your head. Also, beware that you don't become tarnished with the brush of the talentless person you work with. If this boss's reputation rubs off on you, you may find it hard to shake off the stink, which could sabotage your career in the long run. Better to move on if you can't manage to receive individual credit for your work.

HOW TO WORK FOR A CLUELESS INCOMPETENT

When you work with a CI you need to be sure to document everything. Document your efforts to encourage your boss to do his or her share; document what you've done to clean up any mistakes; document work that you've produced that he or she has taken credit for. The best way to document these events is through e-mail to your boss and at least one other person, if appropriate. Why e-mail? Because you can prove that your boss received it. Don't copy everyone on the team if there's no reason to do so—that will only look too obvious and annoy them. Do try to find at least one other person to whom you can e-mail documentation of your attempts to do your job.

Devils Incarnate (DIs)

DIs might not actually be evil, but they certainly do a good imitation of that state; manipulative, overbearing, demanding, and demeaning, they make the other problem bosses pale in comparison. And yet, sometimes a bad boss is simply a bad fit. Just as certain people and personalities are not a match to you as friends, lovers, or spouses, so too, certain personalities are not a match to you as a boss. One golden rule of work is to be who you are, and respect who your boss is. If the fit is excruciating, you need to bail.

One of my first bosses after law school had a devil reputation if there ever was one; however, we worked together like

Bonnie and Clyde, stealing the treasures of our opponents with skill and style. Yet many people quaked in their boots (or Pradas) at the thought of entering his lair. He would get indignant with frustration: "The associates think that I'm the prince of f---ing darkness." I laughed when he said it—twenty years after I started working with him—but I felt his pain . . . and theirs!

The golden key here was *fit*: I was sassy and raised by my father to take no prisoners. When the DI tried to steamroll and abuse me in one of our first encounters (yelling profanities at me in front of a client for a mistake I did not make) my response was a version of, "Hello! You talkin' to me?"

Luckily, I knew my boundaries. I knew I would rather wait tables than work with someone who acted that way. I spoke my piece in true John Wayne fashion (talk straight and shoot straight) and he—surprised to be confronted by someone so new and a female, to boot!—backed off. We had lots of disagreements and discussions, but he never treated me that way again.

I was also lucky in that I was a "do not sweat the small stuff" individual and loved humor. My boss had a temper and charm in equal measure, and could always be joked out of a bad mood if you had the right touch. Luckily, my no-nonsense attitude was a match to his demanding (to put it mildly) style. My DI remains a friend and mentor to me today, years after I left the firm.

WORKING FOR THE DEVILS INCARNATE

But here, dear reader, is where you must assess your own DI carefully. In order to put up with this kind of boss, you need to know whether the DI is merely good at what he or she does or hit-the-ball-out-of-the-park GREAT! If not the latter, then, as the Spanish famously say, *no vale la pena!* It's not worth the pain.

In *The Devil Wears Prada*, the character of Miranda is fabulously modeled after the legendary *Vogue* Editor Anna Wintour, who ate her assistants for breakfast. These women were not stupid; they were the best and brightest in their field. They put up with her abuse and unreasonable demands because she was superb at what she did, and enduring the pain of working with her could catapult their careers. My own DI was recently rated number one in his field by an informal poll of attorneys in our city. I learned things from him that have served me through two other careers. I'll always be grateful for his help and advice.

"How high are you willing to jump?" is *the* question you must constantly process if you work for a brilliant DI. Don't lose yourself or your ideals in the bargain, but do take what you can get—which may be substantial if you can stand the heat. Be careful, however; like the proverbial frog in pan of water that's slowly coming to a boil, you may not notice you're cooked until it's way too late. Sympathy for the devil does not involve sticking with the devil so long that the job dissolves who you are and want to be. Take what you need and leave the rest. Vote with your feet when you can't continue to manage the dynamic and hold on to your soul. Just don't give up too soon. As I explained in Chapter 2, the *Star Wars* series brilliantly reminds us that when we're looking at Darth Vader, we may be staring into the evil eyes of our own father, who has crossed over to the dark side but was once the prince of peace.

Remember also that bosses, like other mere mortals, may also be suffering from personal problems, illness, or other mood and character disorders. If you have such a boss, you have my sympathy. However, be careful not to stay so long that it damages your self-esteem or your sanity. Your own health is more important than any job. You can fire your boss by choosing to walk away and out the door.

If you are the boss, you may be thinking that *employees* are the real problems. Never fear, we'll help with your challenges in the next chapter.

YOUR RELATIONSHIP TOOLBOX

HOW TO MOVE FROM PISSED OFF TO POWERFUL

PISSED OFF	POWERFUL
Whining about the boss	Recognizing that the boss is the boss
Telling off the boss	Skillfully requesting behavior changes
Allowing true abuse	Setting clear bounds for unacceptable behavior
Hiding out	Communicating what you're doing at work
Talking to your friends about actionable behavior	Going to HR or a higher authority

08.
THE MANAGERS' BILL OF RIGHTS

How to outflank the difficult employee.

Brian's underlings squabble more than his four-year-old triplets. Everything's a battle, and it doesn't matter how petty. "They'd fight over paper clips," he fumes. He feels powerless to manage these highly competent engineers. After all, many of them are world-class technical experts, sometimes understanding more about the subject than he. Their behavior, however, has him at his wits' end. What's a frustrated manager with a work force of children to do?

Managers Have Rights, as well as Responsibilities

With all the employment litigation and general employee grousing these days, it can be easy for a manager or supervisor to feel as if he or she is under siege. Employees complain at the first opportunity about workload, their coworkers, and the "lies" they believe upper management is telling them.

In modern workplaces, where just answering e-mail can take up half of all your productive hours, it's easy to lose sight of the big picture: You are the boss. If you're a manager or supervisor, you do have rights. These rights can and should help you manage difficult employees. Your rights are limited to three, but they're big ones! You have the right to:

1. Require compliance with your directives
2. Change standards and assignments
3. Require excellence

Let's take those one at a time.

REQUIRE COMPLIANCE WITH YOUR DIRECTIVES

As long as what you're asking your employees to do isn't illegal, immoral, or unethical, they must do what you ask. Otherwise, it's insubordination. This legal term doesn't just refer to military service; it's a hallmark of employment law: Employees must do what you ask, and if they don't, they can be fired or disciplined. Don't wimp out!

In addition to rights, employees also have responsibilities. One of them is that they must learn to work well with others. In the case of Brian's quarreling engineers, for example, I advised him to direct *them* to learn how to cooperate. You, as a manager, can tell all your difficult employees that they must work well with others. If they don't know how, you can send them to class, buy them books or CDs, or bring in an expert facilitator, but the bottom line is that cooperation is a mandatory skill.

With warring employees, you sometimes just have to lock them into a room until they figure it out. If you're going to try this, you should send in a facilitator or other conflict management expert. What you should *not* do is make cooperation and civil behavior your responsibility when it's clearly theirs.

CHANGE STANDARDS AND ASSIGNMENTS

Employees frequently balk and become difficult when you try to change standards or assignments: "My previous manager didn't make me do that." You may be tempted to reply, "Do I look like your previous manager?" and perhaps you should, but the bottom line is, you can have your own standards, as long as they're legal, ethical, and consistent with your organization's policies.

One manager, Sarah, came to me when she acquired a new team that had very little discipline. Their last manager had been lax. Thus, projects were turned in late, workers pointed fingers at each other, people worked odd hours or not at all, and gossip ran rampant. "How can I convince them to change when they've had such bad management?" she cried.

I advised Sarah that she could and should start fresh. They won't like the change and it won't be easy, I told her, but you need to make it clear that things will be different going forward and you must lay out specific expectations.

One easy way to do this, if you're a new supervisor or gain new employees who appear to be difficult, is to have one-on-ones with each employee in which you set forth your goals, standards, and objectives. Then send them away and have them e-mail back to you their understanding of what you said. Trust me, you'll be depressed. You'll think that human communication is hopeless, because what comes back will be different from what you think you said. You can, however, use this as the opportunity to correct their misconceptions. It also demonstrates that you bent over backward in trying to communicate with them and be fair.

After they've been working for you for a while, you should continue to have these one-on-ones with them. Again, ask them to e-mail back their understanding of what you said.

Again, you'll despair, and think they're speaking a different language. However, if you persevere in correcting these miscommunications, you'll have an excellent documentation trail in which they did most of the work. This also makes writing performance reviews much easier.

REQUIRE EXCELLENCE

Employees cannot get away with sloppy, substandard work. You have a right to insist on performance standards, and you should. As long as you've clearly explained what behavior (not attitude, or other vague term) you need from employees, they must conform to your standards.

Employees' Responsibilities

Just as you have rights, your employees have responsibilities. They must:

- Show up for work on time
- Perform their jobs with reasonable care
- Work well with others
- Give their undivided loyalty to the company

If you have employees who are not doing these things, they're not just difficult—they are failing to meet performance standards. You have a right to coach, counsel, and warn them. If they don't shape up, you can put them on a performance improvement plan and ultimately terminate them if necessary.

Managers' Responsibilities

Likewise, managers have the responsibility to:

- Give employees honest and specific performance feedback
- Set expectations and standards
- Follow the laws and company policies
- Be honest and fair
- Document events
- Be open to employee feedback

The first five standards are based on the law; the last is not, but is very good management and will save you a world of hurt.

DOCUMENTING AND FEEDBACK

Of this list, the most difficult are documenting events and giving performance feedback. If you don't learn these skills, managing difficult people will continue to be difficult.

When you're documenting or giving performance feedback, you should make your feedback and documentation specific and factual, not based upon your conclusions, biases, and assumptions. Here's what I mean:

CONCLUSIONS	FACTS
Your attitude sucks	You failed to answer the phone on time five times and arrived late every day
You're incompetent	You need to learn the new computer program and take a class on project management
You're angry	You yelled at a customer and slammed the door

The difficult people that you manage may not be able to change who they are, but they may change their behavior if you consistently coach and counsel them in the correct way. Most managers wimp out when it comes to giving their employees honest and specific feedback. You're not doing them or the organization any favors if you do this, because they'll never improve their performance and you'll have the headache of dealing with a persistently difficult employee.

LISTENING TO FEEDBACK

Managers often don't want to hear this: You'll never be a successful manager unless you learn how to take feedback from your employees, including negative feedback. You may not like what they have to say, but there's no way to improve your workplace without listening to employee complaints.

For example, I was asked to conduct a team-building session for one of my manufacturing clients. We decided to do an employee survey to find out the issues. The main one was that the manager refused to hear negative news because she saw her team as "the best team ever." It was an admirable sentiment; however, her attitude ensured that she didn't hear things that she needed to hear, since everyone was afraid to bring her problems.

As a manager, you have certain legal and non-legal obligations. You aren't legally required to listen to your employees' feedback or complaints. However, it's impossible to get your employees to face their own problem behavior if you won't do the same.

Many of the other techniques in this book will work for managers dealing with difficult employees, but I hope that this chapter has helped you shore up your own sense that you do have a right to manage difficult employees effectively. In the next chapter, we'll tackle those crabby clients.

YOUR RELATIONSHIP TOOLBOX

HOW TO MOVE FROM PISSED OFF TO POWERFUL

PISSED OFF	POWERFUL
Wimping out	Recognize that you are the boss
Failing to document poor performance	Asking the employees to e-mail back their understanding of your directives
Slacking off on your responsibilities	Being responsible
Hiding your head in the sand	Listening to feedback

09.
HOW TO AVOID KILLING OUTRAGEOUS CLIENTS

Serving a royal pain in the ass.

It was one of those high-maintenance clients: Everyone has one or two. Calling with stupid questions, changing plans at the last minute, asking for advice and then ignoring my suggestions. The latest debacle had been that one of my trainers (Bernice) had been "brusque" with the assistant (Katie) of my client contact (Meredith). The backstory is that I and all of my eight trainers were royally fed up with Katie's incompetence and slothful attitude. However, keeping in mind that my mantra is "the client is the client," we had all sucked it up and done our duty. Bernice, in a fit of exasperation and having a bad day to boot, had unintentionally snapped at Katie over how she had messed up arranging Bernice's travel plans yet once again. Meredith was calling to tell me that she never wanted Bernice to work at any of their locations again.

"Fine," I muttered under my breath into the phone, "and you can add the rest of us to the list because we're all fed up with her and you!"

"What did you say?" Meredith croaked.

I took a deep breath, tried to calm down, and silently repeated to myself, "The client is always right . . . the client is always right . . . the client . . ."

Stand Your Ground Without Losing the Client

How do you negotiate with a client or customer when you know he or she is being unreasonable? Do you take a hard stand, immediately back down, or duck the issue entirely? Learning to manage difficult clients or customers is an important skill, and one you can master with practice.

With Meredith, for example, I knew that the immediate issue wasn't the real issue. There was a backstory here for both of us, and like a good detective, my job was to find out what Meredith's was, and skillfully reveal my own. I reminded myself that the real problem was not Katie versus Bernice (even though my natural fighter's instinct was to go ahead and step into the ring and defend Bernice's honor). Rather, it was about how Meredith and I were both feeling about deeper issues in the present moment, and how we were treating each other.

JUST BREATHE . . .

Normally, in a conflict with a client, I recommend that you take a time-out to cool down. However, there was no chance for that in this situation, as Meredith was live on the phone and I couldn't think of a credible excuse to duck out. So instead, I started with empathy, always a good tack in any conflict if you can calm down enough to pull it off.

"I am so sorry that Katie had this experience with Bernice," I said. "I've never had these kinds of complaints about her before. Most clients love her."

I pressed further. "Perhaps we could have the two of them sit down and work this out?"

"No! Katie would be mortified; I want Bernice off this project!" said Meredith, now raising her voice.

My own backstory at this point is that I really needed Bernice. I also needed a few minutes to calm down and sort out a strategy.

"Meredith, I'm sorry, I really can't fully concentrate on this right now because I'm in the middle of another project. Please give me a minute to finish it up and I'll call you back."

Even though I'm sure that she was annoyed that I'd stopped her without resolving this matter, sometimes it's more important to take a break and collect your thoughts. Though I risked her temporary annoyance, I thought that was better than saying something thoughtless that I'd live to regret. Many people seem to feel that a conflict needs to be resolved immediately when someone confronts them. Not true. A temporary retreat to mobilize your internal forces may be a much more skillful move.

I had, of course, ignored her very clear request to just drop Bernice, instead acting as if it was a problem to be sorted out. This is a tactful way to buy time, always a good option in any conflict, but especially one with a client. Sometimes, a bit of passive-aggressive behavior can save you!

Turning Adversaries into Partners

Issues like this pop up in everyone's life. It's easy to start treating someone as an adversary when you want and need that person to be your partner. In fact, many conflict specialists, myself included, recommend focusing on turning an *adversary* into a *partner*—viewing the *problem* as a common enemy to be jointly tamed. If you can imagine yourself on the same side as the client or customer and plop the problem on the opposite side of the table from the two of you, and, if you can convince the other person to go along, you'll have a leg up.

Before you do that, you need to make the other person feel really heard, something everyone craves. Frequently, if you can hear what your client is complaining about, at both a superficial level as well as the deeper one, the problem either resolves itself or disappears.

After repeating the *partner, partner, listen, listen* mantra, I called Meredith back. "I'm sorry that I couldn't focus before, but I can now. You have my complete attention. I am so sorry that you had to deal with this thing between Bernice and Katie. I know how busy you are and how difficult it's been to find the personnel to staff this project. I'm sure you need this like a hole in the head."

Notice that I still was avoiding her direct request to kick Bernice off the project—a result that simply would not work for me. Instead, I was inviting her to *disclose* the deeper story: she's too busy, Katie is overwhelmed, she doesn't want to lose her, and they both need this particular project and its ensuing conflicts like a hole in the proverbial head.

"Yeah," she sighed, "it's brutal." Meredith then proceeded to relate her most recent interaction with the CEO over a lawsuit the company had been hit with that had taken up a lot of her time, trying to calm down his hysteria. Meredith added that in addition to serving Meredith and two other attorneys, Katie had the pesky task of running the logistics for the diversity trainings we were conducting for the client at plants all over the country. I kept asking questions to let Meredith vent, something she apparently needed desperately. I continued to ask open-ended questions and just listen, and make sympathetic noises, until she calmed down. Sometimes listening without judgment may be all someone needs.

One of the techniques I used during this exchange was to imagine that I was Meredith: dealing with a burnt CEO, an assistant who lacks people skills, chronically over-extended, having a bad week personally and professionally. In our conflict training, we require students to use this technique to switch sides and tell the story of the conflict from the other person's point of view. While students initially resist these kinds of "acting" exercises, they're always revealing and helpful in allowing them to move a conflict that's "stuck."

Seeing Meredith's side made me feel uncomfortable, but also less entitled and less inclined to climb into the ring to defend Bernice's honor. If I did that, I knew I would push Meredith into her corner of the ring, leaving her with no choice but to defend Katie. That result would not serve anyone.

Understanding what someone else is feeling and thinking is a crucial step to resolving conflicts with clients—or anyone else. There is power in our own attitude. Even if someone initially resists our invitation to begin a dialogue, we don't have to react in kind. We can continue to say and do things that turn us into partners. All it takes is persistence in trying to understand the other person's point of view and reflecting it back so that he or she feels that someone understands and appreciates the problems. We can choose to view this as an interesting challenge or a pesky chore.

I listened to Meredith go on until she seemed to wind down, and then I asked, "What would be the best outcome for you for this project?"

This question took her aback and stopped her in her tracks. Until then, she had not been looking at the big picture, but only today's annoyance: the Katie/Bernice row. "Well, the project has had a good outcome so far," she sighs. "It's been a real feather in my cap with the CEO, and I have you to thank for that."

"What if," I suggested, "I talk to Bernice and make sure that she treats Katie with more respect and I will make sure to remind everyone else to do the same. Or, we can use Bernice only if we really need her. Last, but not least, I could talk with Katie directly about Bernice's travel plans, so that she doesn't even have to deal with Bernice."

"Oh, never mind," Meredith said. "I guess it's not such a big deal. Look, I have to run. I'm late for a meeting."

Not all client or customer clashes play out this easily, of course, but the same steps I followed can be used in virtually any customer conflagration. Try this format:

1. Calm yourself down so you can think. Ignore whatever trash they're throwing at you.
2. Focus on the big picture. What is the outcome you really need and want?
3. Find out their backstory. Gradually reveal your own.
4. Ask open-ended questions. Use this format: listen, question, listen, question, listen.
5. Imagine yourself in their shoes, whether they're Gap or Galliano. Articulate their deeper issues, either to yourself, or to them, if appropriate.
6. Brainstorm a solution that meets everyone's needs.

Avoid Getting in the Ring with a Client

Not taking it personally is the key to resolving customer conflicts if you deal with customer service. I remember learning this years ago from an airline customer service rep. Like most frequent flyers, I have my own list of flying horror stories. At this point, I rarely get outraged at whatever airline insanity is going on since I know that I have no control over whether planes take off on time, baggage is lost, or the security line is crawling, but that wasn't always the case.

Back in the 1980s, my then husband and I were headed out on a long-delayed diving vacation to Belize. We were both stressed at work and home and were delighted to be finally taking off for a week of freedom. Of course, the inevitable happened: our luggage was lost in Miami. The stress of the past couple of months got to me and I blew up, along the lines of "how the @#$%&* could you do this to us!"

My reaction, in fact, was so over the top that I was referred to the manager, who walked us down the hall to her office. I continued my harangue as we walked. "One of the things I'm so upset about is we're going to this really remote island off the coast of Belize and even if you find our bags they'll never be able to get them to us on time" and on and on.

She made sympathetic noises as I continued and never lost her cool, or her professionalism. Finally, I calmed down enough to be impressed. "How do you manage to stay so calm with irate travelers lambasting you all day?" I asked.

She shrugged. "I have just learned to never take it personally." Clearly, this is the golden rule of sorting out customer problems.

As I did with Meredith, the key is to understand that it's their problem, not your fault. Your joint goal is to find a solution, not attack back.

Admittedly, it's not always easy to avoid taking someone's behavior personally, especially if they're attacking you. Again, if *you* can focus on the *problem,* not you or them as a person, it's easier. You are a team and you're jointly attacking the issue, which you've skillfully placed opposite the two of you. If they're emotional or attacking, it's because of their deeper issues, which like a good detective you can investigate and find. Then you can both focus on the most positive outcome for both sides.

Once in a While You Just Need to Fire a Client

When do you throw in the towel? Marriage experts hold forth that the three A's—abuse, adultery, and alcohol—are grounds to give up on any marriage. It's a good rule for customers as well.

ABUSE

No one should have to abide abuse at work. One time, if it's not severe, is understandable. But after a warning, if someone is still doing the same thing, give it up. I'm not talking about a few raised voices or less-than-felicitous words here; I'm talking about a continual crossing of boundaries that makes you miserable. Screaming, profanity, and certainly physical abuse all are over the line. You need to complain to your manager, HR, their manager, and even call 911 if they're abusing you and won't leave the premises.

A friend of mine owns a store that sells discount motorcycle gear. One day a would-be patron came in obviously inebriated, waving a beer bottle and threatening to kill one of his sales clerks. She ran to the bar next door and called 911. Clearly, such behavior is over the line.

But what about less obvious behavior? Yelling, temper tantrums, name calling. Everyone has their own personal limit but mine is this: If you listen sympathetically to their tirade and they still continue when you've asked them to stop, that's it. Call your security people or the police. No one should feel threatened at work. You are irreplaceable. Customers are not.

ALCOHOL OR SUBSTANCE ABUSE

Clearly, if someone is under the influence of alcohol or drugs, you shouldn't have to deal with them and the same rules apply as those for dealing with abuse: Ask them to stop and if they don't, you leave and call for help. Be careful, however, since it is possible that certain medical conditions can mimic alcohol problems.

I once had a plumber collapse into a diabetic coma in my house. Luckily, he was training someone else, so the newbie helped me get him to the couch and pour some juice into his mouth. Despite his objections, I called 911. If his partner hadn't known what was happening, I would have sworn the plumber was drunk.

ADULTERY

While you won't deal with adultery per se with a client or customer, I have seen many sexual harassment (or racial, ethnic, age, etc.) incidents with clients or customers. You should not have to put up with sexual innuendos, unwelcome requests for sexual favors, or sexual or racial epithets at work. Even if this behavior is being directed at you by an outside client or customer, your employer must create a safe environment for its employees. If this happens, tell your manager or HR. If they won't listen, call the Equal Employment Opportunity

Commission (EEOC) or the state Fair Employment Practices board.

The law is on your side on this one. (As is, most likely, your employer's policy.) Your employer has an obligation to provide a work environment that's free from harassment. Even though the company may not be able to control the behavior of cussing customers, it can control the environment, forcibly evicting the offenders if need be.

More Techniques to Soothe Beastly Customers

Before you pull the plug on a pugnacious customer or client, consider these additional techniques. First, allow him or her to express anger and resentment appropriately. Let the person speak these feelings until he or she is finished. Acknowledge the feelings, which means listening and sympathizing *without* excuses or explanations. He or she is trying to get complete about the past, meaning that this situation and/or you are reminding him of some past upset and they're taking it out on you. Reassure him or her that you will not allow the past to repeat itself in this relationship. If you let the person completely express all of his or her feelings, anger and resentment will turn into appreciation.

Appreciation is also a good way to keep clients or customers from turning into a pain in the butt. Frequently ask them, "What can I do that would make you feel more appreciated today?" Wow! What a question. Can you imagine how you'd feel if the businesses you patronize asked you this question instead of taking you for granted? Customer service issues would evaporate.

Marriott International, Inc., which is highly regarded around the world for its customer service, makes certain that its managers live and die by its GSIs (guest service indexes). If the GSI sinks too low at any property, the manager must go! Don't you wish everyone had this standard? Customers would be a happier lot.

The Power of Silence

If you're on the receiving end of a customer harangue, try something new: the power of silence. If you've never used silence to make a point, you don't understand how powerful this communication tool can be. Being able to use the sound of silence is one of the greatest conversational arts. Our ability to be quiet may confirm that we are intensely interested in what is being said. It can also show that we have great integrity and will not be brought into conversations that could be demeaning. Ben Franklin said, "Remember not only to say the right thing in the right place, but far more difficult still, to leave unsaid the wrong thing at the tempting moment." Silence allows us to keep a secret, to serve as a peacemaker, and to learn the deeper meaning about what is being said.

Have you ever been in a conversation in which all you were waiting for was for the speaker to pause, so that you could interject your reply? Instead of allowing ourselves to pause and absorb what has been said, we start preparing how we want to vocalize our thoughts as soon as the speaker stops talking. That is not listening; it is merely practicing our next speech.

Realize that there will always be some people who misunderstand or misinterpret your silence. Some people will take your pause as a time to jump into the conversation by engaging their mouth. When we do speak, our brains should be fully engaged so that our words are clear and easily understood.

Otherwise our words are only noise pollution. Silence is a powerful sword. We can use silence to increase our understanding and learn more about the people around us. When used out of compassion, it can show that we care deeply enough to listen with the intent to understand.

However, the other side of the silence sword can cut through the air when our intent is to hurt or let someone know we are displeased. Dead silence can cause a conversation to feel heavy, because the speaker may not know whether he or she was heard or understood. The art of silence is learned. When we are accustomed to noise, we may mistake silence for lack of understanding. How loud is your silence speaking with the people you serve? Is your silence allowing you to hit your mark and better understand your clients, or are you using it to dismiss, intimidate, or punish passive-aggressively? Be aware of your intentions with this tactic.

So the next time you're confronted by a really troublesome client or customer, try silence. Simply let the person talk, vent, even rage to their heart's content. If he or she is behaving like a snarling, snapping, sniping pit bull, realize that most pit bulls are like balloons full of hot air: if you simply allow them to go on long enough, they'll eventually deflate.

If the person pauses, ask another open-ended question, starting with who, what, where, or when. If you can't think of anything else to say, you can always just simply ask, "And then what happened?" Every time the client or customer runs through the problem at hand, you can help him or her blow off the anger until it disappears. In between the tirades, use the power of silence.

Managing crusty customers and clients can be hard work. You need the support of all your coworkers to succeed. You'll find customers or clients impossible if you're working with slackers, know-it-alls, or people who explode. In the next chapter, we'll cover techniques to manage them.

YOUR RELATIONSHIP TOOLBOX

HOW TO MOVE FROM PISSED OFF TO POWERFUL

PISSED OFF	POWERFUL
Blowing up at a difficult client or customer	Calming yourself down
Cutting off their emotions	Allowing them to ventilate
Accepting the client/customer view of the problem	Inviting them to disclose the underlying issue
Getting sucked into the details of the complaint	Seeking the big-picture outcome
Meeting your own needs	Finding a solution that meets everyone's needs
Talking too much	Listening

10.

HOW TO NAVIGATE ROAD RAGERS, SLACKERS, AND WHINERS

You talkin' to me?

Linda and Nancy have been colleagues for years. Yet Linda is about at the end of her rope with Nancy's know-it-all nitpicking. A typical conversation goes something like this:

Linda: "We need to talk about our strategy for the new ad campaign."

Nancy: "First we need to decide on the paper color. I've found that we can save ten cents on flyers if we use pink instead of blue; last time you didn't even consider pink!"

Linda: "Before we get to paper, I'd like to agree on the big idea behind the campaign."

Nancy: "But we have to decide about the paper today, the sale ends tomorrow. I found out that if we order online we have until midnight, and we can save an additional ten cents per ream if we use UPS instead of FedEx, and if you authorize it right now I can get our order in before noon which means they could deliver it . . ."

Linda: "Stop with the paper already! We need to deal with the bigger issues first."

Nancy: "Of course. I understand that getting the details right isn't as important to you as it is to me. Don't worry. I'll just handle it myself."

Linda: (Fights every urge to throttle the living daylights out of Nancy.)

The Know-It-All

Know-it-alls will drive you absolutely batty. They're the employees, colleagues, or bosses who think it's their place to do your job as well as their own. Their condescending tone and attitude is present in every conversation and interpersonal exchange. Still can't spot them? They're the ones who seem to want to be back in fourth grade, where they used to sit in the front row, furiously waving their hand, while insistently whining, "Call on me, call on me, call on me!"

Some people just can't keep themselves from telling you, and everyone else, what they know. (And they know *everything*.) They seem to think that you need their information now, whether or not their information pertains to the subject currently being discussed.

HOW TO HANDLE A KNOW-IT-ALL

Know-it-alls are in some ways contradictory: They want to feel superior, which often alienates them from peers and colleagues, yet at the same time they also crave being needed. It helps if you can use these people; for example, get them on projects that take up all their time. They'll be convinced that what they're doing is oh-so-important. It may also distract them enough to get them off your back.

I used to work with an attorney named Janice who truly did seem to know everything. This was in the dark ages before everyone kept subject files on the computer. She kept vast subject files on various legal issues in her desk. Everyone knew that you should start your research at Janice's desk, not in the library. Luckily, she was generous with her time and advice.

Many times, if someone like this pisses us off, it's because of our own fears and inadequacies, not because of what they're doing. Know-it-alls can be very competent, particularly with minutiae most people dismiss; thus, Janice sometimes rubbed people the wrong way because her extraordinary thoroughness highlighted others' weaknesses. Use know-it-alls on projects for which details are critical: they'll relish the role.

Other times, know-it-alls can be an unnecessary pain in the process, and in your backside. Once, near the end of my tenure as a litigation attorney, I inadvertently left something off a pre-trial filing. Instead of filing a motion to ask the court if I could add it, I simply called the young opposing attorney to ask for her permission. Before granting the request, she put me through an inquisition! "Why did you not include this in your previous filing?" she kept asking in various ways.

"Because we made a mistake," I responded casually. This seemed to inflame her suspicion. She could not believe that we had simply made a mistake, and hadn't orchestrated it for some other nefarious purpose. Round and round we went. Finally, I gave up and filed a request with the court, which was, as most such routine requests were, routinely granted. I am fairly certain that the reason she had trouble understanding the whole exchange was that she was a classic know-it-all who believed that *she* would never make such a mistake and thus felt justified questioning my motives and creating unnecessary work. In situations like this, your only option may be to grit your teeth (as I did) and jump through the hoop.

WHAT DRIVES THE KNOW-IT-ALL?

People who are the workplace know-it-all have the need to feel in control of their environment, usually as a way of medicating their own anxiety about their inadequacies. Since you are in their environment, that includes controlling you too. This can be annoying, even enraging, if you're the constant victim of all this "helping." Again, the best way to deal with these bozos is to do your best to not take it personally. Ignore their behavior whenever you can, unless it has an impact on team or group performance. If it does have an impact on performance, you need to do your best to confront the issue skillfully and then to complain to your supervisor or HR if you don't get results.

The detail-oriented know-it-all

Many know-it-alls have high IQs but such low EQs (levels of emotional intelligence) that they actually think people admire them for saying things like, "We can save ten cents on paper" when you're still trying to nail down the big idea for a multimillion-dollar ad campaign. Detail-oriented know-it-alls don't sit around memorizing amazing facts. Instead they correct others' versions of events, often missing the whole point of a conversation in their obsessive focus on minutiae.

Detail-oriented know-it-alls can sustain conversations for inordinate amounts of time—all the while being oblivious to the irritation their monologue is engendering in those who are held hostage to it. Most of the time, work colleagues simply talk over them, though if you have a detail-oriented know-it-all in the next cube it helps to have earplugs available for emergencies.

Fixer know-it-alls

Another typical know-it-all behavior is that they insist on solving your problems for you, even if you don't want them solved, or, in fact, don't think you have a problem at all. Fixer know-it-alls will persist in making recommendations, despite your best efforts to derail them. Even if you're just venting, they will relish solving the problem. For example, when you're musing about your marriage, she'll suggest a new vitamin.

If you know you're right on the facts and they're wrong, you can try to out-brain the brainiacs. This frequently leads to an all-out battle of the brains, however. A better way than wading into the IQ challenge is to approach the know-it-all at the level of EQ. Know-it-alls are weak as puppies in this area, so be gentle. In a soft, nonaggressive tone, say, "Pat, I think you're showing off your knowledge to get acceptance. The thing is, that really doesn't work. I just feel annoyed when you harp on information I never asked for."

It's always a good idea to put know-it-alls to work, doing what they do best. Know-it-alls want most of all to be of service. Recognize their offensive behaviors for what they are—manifestations of insecurity—and put them to work diagnosing your computer glitch, balancing the department's budget, or figuring out why your janitor doesn't empty the trash cans. No project is too big or too small for the typical know-it-all. What you don't want is these people sitting around without a project, which just leads to them spending all their time critiquing your work. Instead, keep a list of all the work stuff you loathe and hand it off!

You Snooze, You Lose: Shake Up Those Slackers

Hate working with slackers? You're in good company. In a recent study by Leadership IQ, a training and research company based in Washington, D.C., 87 percent of employees said that working beside low-performing colleagues had made them want to change jobs. Further, 93 percent also claimed that working with low performers decreased their productivity.

"Low performers can feel like emotional vampires, sucking the energy out of everyone around them," said Leadership IQ chief executive Mark Murphy, whose company surveyed 70,305 employees, managers, and executives from 116 companies and organizations. Those surveyed were asked to list characteristics of a low performer. The top five characteristics were:

1. A negative attitude
2. A tendency to stir up trouble
3. Often blames others
4. Lacks initiative
5. Is incompetent

Low performers are often skilled in the art of work avoidance. They spend more time arguing their way out of tasks than it would take to simply complete them. They are good at identifying problems but not so good at finding solutions. They have well-crafted excuses for not getting anything done. And their sloth is often at the expense of more conscientious coworkers, who must pick up their slack.

Ironically enough, many slackers do not see themselves as slackers, preferring instead to blame others. Of the 87 percent of employees who want to get away from low performers, half are probably low performers themselves, if other surveys can be believed. For instance, more than half of American workers are not engaged in their jobs, according to a recent survey by Gallup. Most are "sleepwalking through their workdays," Gallup says. But 19 percent are what Gallup calls the "actively disengaged." The 23 million "actively disengaged" U.S. workers cost the national economy more than 300 billion a year in lost productivity.

DEALING WITH SLACKERS

In short, if companies hope to keep their best employees, they should dump their worst. Otherwise, low performers will start dictating the company's culture; productivity, quality, and service will all decline precipitously, and high performers will avoid your company like the plague.

Former General Electric CEO Jack Welch fired the bottom 10 percent of his work force each year. Welch used sports metaphors to justify this extreme practice, saying he wanted to work with A-team performers. He was roundly criticized as callous, but GE did flourish under his management. "I think the cruelest thing you can do to somebody is give them a head fake . . . nice appraisals . . . that's called false kindness," writes Welch in the book *The Jack Welch Lexicon of Leadership*.

Most managers avoid addressing the problem of poor performers. When I teach management classes, for example, I routinely ask how many of them have someone on a performance improvement plan. Usually only 1 or 2 percent of them do, despite surveys that show at least 20 percent of the employees in any workplace perform poorly.

There's plenty of false kindness and management wimpiness going around. In the Leadership IQ survey, only 14 percent of senior executives said their company effectively managed low performers. And only 17 percent of middle managers said they feel comfortable removing low performers.

Slackers can be pretty intimidating to most leaders. A lot of managers simply don't want to deal with them. They will duck down a side hallway just to avoid engagement. Managers avoid slackers for many reasons. Some may lack the skills to manage performance effectively. Performance management is difficult and requires a manager to make certain that he or she knows what behavior constitutes acceptable performance.

Many managers really do not know what the criteria should be, beyond counting "face time" in the office.

Other managers may be paranoid about confronting an employer who is different from them in some way: a different gender, race, or generation. Finally, many managers don't want to make anyone feel bad, or they lack confrontation skills.

Can slackers be fired for goofing off at work? Ask the hapless New York City clerk fired by Mayor Michael Bloomberg for being discovered playing a game of solitaire when Bloomberg and a group of reporters trooped into the clerk's office on a tour. Bloomberg canned him on the spot, which is legal if employees have been warned that such behavior isn't allowed. (After all, you are supposed to work at work.)

What to do about slackers? Document, document, document. If the lazy bum is a coworker, make sure your boss knows that you're doing your part. If your boss is the culprit, e-mail memos to him or her confirming all conversations so that you can make it clear to anyone who investigates down the road that you've done your part.

Road Ragers—Preventing Spontaneous Combustion On Your Team

Do you have team members who are constantly angry? Anything sets them off: the copier isn't working, someone forgot to make coffee, their e-mail disappeared into cyberspace, they don't like the way you breathe. Whatever it is, they fuss, fume, and scream at routine, daily annoyances that the rest of us grin and bear. Why do they do that?

When people are angry about everything, the critical common denominator is *them*. They mistakenly think anger is empowering and rage is a way of being assertive. Nothing could be further from the truth. When someone is constantly irritated, they're assuming the "poor me" victim role, which is the weakest posture one can take. In most instances, anger is nothing more than an outward manifestation of a very different underlying emotion. A colleague who regularly exhibits anger is probably scared, hurt, frustrated, or a combination of the three. Anger may also be a mask for depression. Often, those suffering from depression don't simply withdraw; they may also strike out against others in frustration. If this is the case, it helps to understand and treat this colleague with compassion.

This doesn't mean, however, that you should take abuse. Abuse should never be tolerated in the workplace—or anywhere else for that matter. Walk away; complain to your boss or HR; and document, document, document. Just be sure that you document *behavior*—specifically what they say or do—not your conclusions, assumptions, or biases about the person's behavior.

As you learned in Chapter 4, there is also a subtle thing that can happen in groups called emotional contagion. Because we're social animals, we have evolved in a way that makes our brains resonate with others. When this happens, we are affected by the mood that's occurring in the brains of those with whom we interact. This brain contagion actually helps us, in that we're then able to "read" the moods of others and, perhaps, respond more appropriately based upon those moods. If someone is angry, for example, we may choose to keep our distance. If someone is sad or anxious, our natural tilt toward compassion might kick in, and we might be moved to comfort or help them in some way.

What's startling about the latest research is that when our brains connect at this moment, we are not only moved to try to help or avoid the other person, but our own brains are literally changed in response.

This recent science underscores what we all know instinctively. If the boss walks into a meeting fussing and fuming, everyone else's mental health and mood may be affected. Conversely, if one of your gloomy peers walks into a meeting unhappy, the power of the group may buoy this person. The group brain can overpower the individual temper, while the boss's power may cancel out your individual moods.

DEALING WITH RAGERS

So there are very practical reasons for limiting your exposure to others' toxic brains. And, of course, if you can't limit your exposure, you need to file a complaint, or even change jobs if the abuse persists and cannot be stopped. This is especially true if the person exhibits any of the warning signs of violence, as discussed in Chapter 3. If he or she does, you need to complain immediately. One way of confronting a person who is habitually angry is to say something like this:

"You did _____." (Describe specifically what the person said or did.)

"When I objected to your behavior, you ignored me." (Or yelled, etc.; describe what the person did.)

"I care about you and support you and I wish you success in our workplace, but if we're going to work together you need to treat me and the other members of our team with respect." (Set a boundary with the abuser.)

"You hurt me (or them) when you said or did _____. It also resulted in us missing a key deadline because Mary was so

upset by your outburst that she had to go home and thus the assignment wasn't completed." (Describe the behavior and the result of that behavior upon yourself, your colleagues, and the work itself.)

"I would hope this is something you're not proud of. If you want to continue to stomp around with a frown on your face, go ahead, but you're going to do it without us." (Outline consequences of repeating the behavior.)

"I respect your work and I want to have a good working relationship with you, but peace at any price is no peace at all. You owe me and the team an apology. I intend to give you the benefit of the doubt and move past this, but we've had our last heated argument and I've taken my last bit of abuse from you." (Add a specific request and repeat that you will not tolerate the behavior.)

The most important thing to remember is that this conversation takes place in person—not via e-mail. Talk with the individual directly and privately, listen to his or her response (and ideally, an apology) and then you can confirm what you both said with an e-mail. This is a good way to document behavior, as well as your attempts to communicate about a person's behavior, in case you need to escalate your complaints to a manager, HR, or an attorney. Before you take any of this action, however, take the advice of St. Francis and seek first to understand. If we understand why people do what they do, it helps us to make sense of their behavior, have more compassion for it, and slow down our own reactivity. If we're grounded in our thinking brain, we are better able to be effective with someone who is highly emotional and out of control than we would be if we just followed their lead and spewed all over the place at them.

Zookeeping the Animals in Your Workplace

With all these different kinds of problem children, you might try the techniques wild-animal trainers employ with such great success! Writer Amy Sutherland spent a year studying with animal trainers. She then wrote a *New York Times* article titled "Kicked, Bitten and Scratched: Life and Lessons at the World Premier School for Exotic Animal Trainers," explaining how she tried the magic techniques on her husband.

What's the secret? The technique is brilliant in its simplicity, although difficult in the discipline required to execute it. You reward the behavior you like and ignore the behavior you don't like. Ms. Sutherland—like most of us with our significant others—had been using the exact opposite technique: Nagging. Once she switched to appreciating her husband for doing things she liked, and ignoring what she loathed, his behavior changed. Sutherland explains:

"After all, you don't get a sea lion to balance a ball on the end of its nose by nagging. The same goes for the American husband.

"Back in Maine, I began thanking Scott if he threw a dirty shirt into the hamper. If he threw in two, I'd kiss him. Meanwhile, I would step over any soiled clothes on the floor without one sharp word, though I did sometimes kick them under the bed. But as he basked in my appreciation, the piles became smaller."

Sutherland used what wild-animal trainers call "approximations," rewarding the small steps toward learning a whole new behavior. Animals don't learn to balance balls in one session, just as she found that husbands don't pick up dirty socks with one reminder.

She also started studying her husband as one would an exotic animal. What are its habits? Diet? Likes? Dislikes? Does it sleep in trees or under benches? You might try the same with a coworker who annoys you. Knowledge is power and the better to train with.

Once you have this information, you can begin to appreciate and reward any movement toward behavior that you want. Say, for example, that you want the slacker in your group to start doing something—anything!—that looks like working instead of surfing porn sites all day. If he picks up a report and starts to read, you would congratulate him on working. If he turns in one project—even if three more remain outstanding—you would applaud and offer him M&M's. You get the idea. Acknowledge any movement toward success, no matter how small, and ignore the rest.

Though they may be effective, applying wild-animal training techniques to the creatures in your particular workplace zoo may challenge your endurance. In that case, see the techniques in the next chapter, which explains how to rearrange your own stress level. If all else fails, consider a nap.

YOUR RELATIONSHIP TOOLBOX

HOW TO MOVE FROM PISSED OFF TO POWERFUL

PISSED OFF	POWERFUL
Blowing up at the know-it-alls	Assigning appropriate work to know-it-alls
Believing know-it-alls act the way they do to be annoying	Understanding that they act the way they do to control their own anxiety
Ignoring slackers	Rewarding work and managing poor performance
Taking abuse	Skillfully confronting ragers

11.
CHILL OUT

How to cope when you want to slap someone.

Betsy Buster roars into work at 7:15 A.M. and starts firing e-mails, voice mails, and verbal rants to any hapless underlings unlucky enough to be within shouting distance. Report reading consumes her nights and weekends, and of course, e-mail never sleeps, nor does she. Breakfast is an Egg McMuffin with cheese that Betsy gobbles while navigating her commute with the aggression of a NASCAR pro. She works through lunch and dines on whatever stale pastries are available in the company kitchen. The last time she took a mental health day was 1994, when she spiked a temperature of 104° and her eyes swelled shut from an infection. Cranky? That's her middle name.

Americans Work Too Much

Americans work almost 200 more hours annually than we did in 1970—that's about an extra month of work a year. According to Juliet B. Schor, a social economist at Boston College and author of *The Overworked American: The Unexpected Decline of Leisure*, putting in long hours isn't necessarily problematic. After all, the rewards of hard work—a fatter paycheck, bonus points with the boss, satisfaction from your accomplishments—abound. It's only when the daily grind eclipses other areas of your life that it's time to stop and rethink your schedule. The reality is this: Everyone you work with will piss you off if you're stressed to the max from overwork and too little self-care.

What Drives Workaholics

According to Bryan E. Robinson, a therapist in Asheville, North Carolina, and author of *Chained to the Desk: A Guidebook for Workaholics, Their Partners and Children, and the Clinicians Who Treat Them*, "Workaholics are out of balance. They don't have many friends. They don't take care of themselves. They don't have any hobbies outside of the office. A hard worker will be at his desk, thinking about the ski slopes. A workaholic will be on the ski slopes thinking about his desk."

According to Robinson, children of parents with emotional problems are often put on the path to workaholism when they must become responsible for their siblings, housework, and sometimes even those checked-out parents. Kids learn that it's much easier to focus on tasks than to deal with painful feelings, a kind of avoidance that's often carried into adulthood. Workaholism, Robinson's research has shown, is closely correlated with the inability to be intimate, and many of his clients enter treatment because their close relationships are falling apart. People who are rigid and perfectionist, or those who are born achievers, are also more likely to morph into workaholics.

After almost two decades of research, Robinson has identified a few different breeds of workaholics. Here's a guide to the different species:

The All-or-Nothing Workaholic: He does things perfectly or not at all. He struggles to get started on projects for fear of not meeting his own impossible expectations. When he does get rolling, he binges to the point of exhaustion. His thinking and his approach to work is all or nothing.

The Relentless Workaholic: These types don't have problems getting started; it's the stopping they have trouble with. They can't say "no," set priorities, or delegate. They may also be people pleasers who don't want to disappoint others.

The Savoring Workaholic: These types obsess over details to the point of paralysis. They hate letting projects go and will often create additional work whenever they get close to finishing a task. They tell themselves that no one could do it as well as they could. They may also be know-it-alls.

Still think that being a workaholic is an advantage? Gayle Porter, management professor at Rutgers University in New Jersey, in her book, *Workaholics as High-Performance Employees: The Intersection of Workplace and Family Relationship Problems*, says, "Workaholics are terrible team players. They allow crisis situations to develop because it makes them look like a hero."

The result is that workaholics often don't get much accomplished. That's why Porter thinks more bosses would do well to reward those who clock out at the end of the day. "The employee who wants to go home is the one who will be most efficient during the week, because she's protecting her time off."

Combating Workaholism

Okay, so what do you do if you're a Type A personality—and you have the stress to show for it? Cut your electronic leashes: Eat lunch out of the office without answering your cell phone. No laptops in bed or at the table. No e-mail on weekends. Other tips to cut the work chains that bind you:

> **Prioritize:** Learn to decide what must come first. It's a way to recognize that some things in life are more important than others. Focus on the big picture in life and at work.

> **Tame Your To-Do List:** Set a cutoff for the number of tasks that can reasonably be accomplished in a day—no more than five. If a new task must be added, knock another off that demands equivalent time. Schedule time for play and relaxation. Also, most time-management experts agree that you need to list not just the tasks, but also how long it will take to accomplish each task. This can change your perception of why you end up at the end of the day with so many things undone.

I remember once taking my impossible to-do list to a professional support group of colleagues so that they could help me figure out why I couldn't get everything finished. They just laughed! One glance at the list revealed to them the truth I'd failed to understand: There was simply no way could I accomplish these tasks in the time allowed. I needed to readjust my expectations of myself and those around me or I was going to be constantly angry with myself and colleagues who couldn't meet my unrealistic standards.

Dire circumstances can push even the most severe workaholics off the treadmill. The hero of the movie *Stranger Than*

Fiction, for example, decided to take a vacation only when he thought his death was imminent: Mortality made him boldly reassess things. Here are a few other signs that you are working too long and too hard:

You're experiencing health problems: Workaholism can contribute to an array of health problems. If that is the case, you need to slow down.

"Dad, Can I Be a Client?": Has your family complained that they never see you? Does time with your spouse have to be scheduled into your Palm Pilot three months in advance? Does your child come home with a drawing of your family that doesn't include you? I'll never forget the day I was packing for yet another business trip and my four-year-old son jumped into my suitcase, asking if he could go with me. That was a wake-up call. Put things in perspective: At the end of your life, you won't wish you'd spent more time at the office.

To slow down, consider the following suggestions.

THE GLORIES OF POWER NAPPING

Americans are a nation of insomniacs; that conclusion is the only one to draw from watching all the sleep aid ads on television. According to the National Sleep Foundation *(www.sleepfoundation.org)*, one-third of us have trouble sleeping some or all of the time; millions take sleep aids or fall asleep at work or on the job. Twenty percent admit to falling asleep while driving.

What's the cause of all this night-owl behavior? Experts point to various causes, including television, computer, and other screen time. There also can be physical causes; for example, sleep apnea, a condition that causes people to stop breathing during sleep, resulting in a net loss of rest, even if they think they're staying in bed the requisite eight hours. Also, we're no longer a nation that rises and rests with the roosters.

Clearly we work more than ever before. And of course, longer commuting time and family demands add to the lack of sleep. Lack of exercise is also a contributing factor; numerous studies show that regular exercise, particularly exercise done outdoors, results in better quality of sleep.

What to do about all this vampire behavior? In a word: surgery. Cut out tasks and commitments that aren't absolutely necessary. Do whatever lifestyle surgery you need in order to get at least eight hours of sleep. Some people need even more, but the average American is clocking in at six and a half. No wonder we're all so cranky! You simply cannot do your best and control your own mood if you're constantly sleep deprived. Lack of sleep makes all of us less than our best and can cause depression and weight gain, in addition to irritability and the feeling that we want to slap someone. So get at least eight hours of sleep; you'll feel much less pissed off if you do!

EAT YOUR GREENS

Is there a mom who doesn't harp about eating your vegetables? Fortunately or unfortunately, Mom was correct! There is no question that good eating—including those vegetables—impacts our mood and performance. If you can keep your mood stable and your body healthy, you'll be better able to deal with those annoying coworkers. Check out the book *Food and Mood*, by Elizabeth Somer and Nancy Snyderman, if you have doubts that your pissed-off state is influenced by what you eat.

We all have our crabby days. Sometimes you can blame it on the weather (a blizzard, a heat wave) or your boss (he's given you a last-minute project) or even the post office (where is that check?). But other times bad moods strike from nowhere—and suddenly, you're snippy with the first person to cross your path. Depressed? Perhaps. But you may just be hungry for the right kind of food.

What and when you eat, even at a single meal, can affect whether you feel happy, sad, irritable, alert, calm, or sleepy. If you pick the wrong foods or skip eating, you may ratchet up your chance of having a stressful or emotional day. Food helps regulate an array of chemicals called neurotransmitters, which circulate throughout the brain, facilitating communication among the hundreds of nerves that help govern your mood.

Serotonin leads the pack in name recognition among these brain chemicals. Low levels of this chemical contribute to many types of depression. Many of the popular antidepressant drugs work by moderating serotonin activity in the brain. Diet also has a profound affect on serotonin secretion. In the absence of certain foods, including protein to produce its precursor, tryptophan, and carbohydrates to trigger its release, serotonin levels can go haywire, leading to irritability and cravings for carbohydrates, which is your brain's way of self-medicating.

Serotonin is just one of the players in the orchestra of brain chemicals that regulate mood. The others include neuropeptide Y (NPY), galanin, dopamine, and the endorphins. In addition, blood sugar levels and certain nutrients, including the B vitamin folate and omega-3 fatty acids, play a role.

If you think that you can go without breakfast and still function, consider the data: Breakfast skippers, on average, score poorly on cognitive and alertness tests, report more hunger throughout the day, and feel more irritable, fatigued, and cranky than do people who feast in the A.M.

Poor diet, little sleep, and lack of exercise can send us into uneven highs and lows that do not help us gain the emotional stability we need. Investigate your diet and lifestyle choices to see whether they're contributing to your road rage in the hallways.

CLEAN LIVING WILL DO YOU GOOD

There's no question that the workplace is more stressful and requires more from us than ever before. The best way to offload that stress is to make sure that you have the best possible health habits and health care. Having a heavy load on your body clearly affects your mind and emotional state. When you're dueling with difficult coworkers, the added stress of dealing with a fading body is just too much for most of us.

Here's a clean-living checklist. If you answer no to any of these questions, it's going to be difficult for you to control your stress well enough to deal with the inevitable people who will piss you off:

1. I have excellent health care. ☐YES ☐NO
2. I sleep at least eight hours but no more than ten every day. ☐YES ☐NO
3. I enjoy caffeine and alcohol in moderation or not at all. ☐YES ☐NO
4. I enjoy the social and emotional support of family and/ or friends. ☐YES ☐NO
5. I have someone to talk to when I'm upset, whose counsel I respect. ☐YES ☐NO
6. I have something I look forward to doing every day. ☐YES ☐NO
7. I enjoy hobbies and my spiritual and social life; work doesn't define me. ☐YES ☐NO

If you answered no to two or more of these questions, no wonder you're pissed off. You need radical lifestyle surgery.

Managing Other Workaholics

What if it's not you who works too much but your boss or workplace colleagues, who then expect you to do the same? How do you cope? In a word: limits. Effective limit-setting is a skill that every worker needs. You have to be crystal clear about what you will give personally and professionally. Of course, the reality is that most of us (unless we're trust-fund babies) need to work; however, you may not need this particular job if it's killing you or you're consistently neglecting your family and friends.

Other chapters of this book contain suggestions about how to communicate limits; here are a few additional suggestions:

1. **Determine your boundaries.** For example, you may be willing to travel away from your kids once a month but not once a week. You may be willing to work one weekend a month but not every one. Talk with your spouse, a therapist, or religious adviser to find out what's realistic for you.

2. **Communicate your limits without judgment.** Once you know what you can and cannot realistically handle, discuss your findings with your boss and *relevant* colleagues (there is no need for the entire office to know). You don't need to cast any aspersions on their sanity or character (in other words, don't belittle them if they choose to be workaholics). Simply communicate what you will and will not do, calmly and without emotion. Here's an example. After several sessions with me, one of my clients went to her boss with her bottom-line

assessment during a business reorganization in which everyone was working too much. "I realize that everyone is stretched thin," she told him, "but I just can't keep doing this. I'm willing to work two jobs, but not three." Surprisingly, he apologized, and rearranged her workload. He had no idea how much she was actually doing.

3. **Keep your boss and relevant coworkers informed.** Sometimes your boss may not really know or understand what you're doing. Find out how your colleagues want to be kept up-to-date (reports, e-mails, face-to-face meetings, and so on) and let them know what you're doing and how long it's taking. They may be surprised to learn how hard you work.

4. **Accept the consequence of doing less.** Life requires painful compromises and choices. Contrary to what Hollywood may imply, nobody is running around out there with a perfect life: impeccable hair, model kids, a high-powered job, a well-behaved dog, and romantic spouse. You need to decide what's most important to you and those you love. If working less results in less money or necessitates a search for another job, the tradeoff may be well worth it.

Be the Ruler of Your World, at Least for a Day

The failure to manage negative emotions drives a continual state of being pissed off, as well as dire health consequences. You need to do whatever it takes to learn how to have a healthy outlet for the big four: anger, sadness, fear, and guilt.

Doubt that? Consider a study that appeared in *Thorax: An International Journal of Respiratory Medicine* (*www.thorax*

.bmj.com). This new research suggests that men who are chronically hostile and angry may face a future of sharply diminished lung function. In 1986, scientists administered a questionnaire to 670 men ages 21 to 80 to assess their hostility. Each then received a pulmonary exam within one year of completing the questionnaire. The men were tracked for an average of 8.22 years, with comprehensive physical examinations every 3 to 5 years, including an average of three pulmonary function tests.

After controlling for age, weight, height, smoking status, and other variables, the scientists found a consistent association between high hostility and lower levels of lung function. Among more hostile men, pulmonary function declined at every exam over a ten-year period when compared with less hostile subjects.

Since levels of lung function were in the normal range at the start of the study, the researchers say, the possibility that poor lung function led to hostility, rather than the other way around, is unlikely. They acknowledge, however, that an unknown factor could cause both hostility and poor lung function.

Still, Dr. Rosalind J. Wright, an assistant professor of medicine at Harvard and the senior author of the study, said there was no doubt that emotions could cause physical changes, some of which could be detrimental. "When you experience physical symptoms around negative emotions, your heart rate goes up, you start sweating, and so on," Dr. Wright said. "Changes in bodily functions—nervous system, immune function—need to occur for you to feel these things. It is possible that similar processes are going on more locally; say in the lungs, which over many years may cause inflammation that affects lung function."

You may also be overscheduling too much, making you chronically anxious. According to online sources such as WebMd and Medline, between 6.5 and 13 percent of the population suffers from anxiety disorders. While this statistic is difficult to track, most practitioners agree that the number of people suffering from anxiety is on the rise. In his book *The Overload Syndrome*, Richard Swenson, MD, explains that Americans schedule their lives at 110 percent, 120 percent, and even higher. Swenson says we no longer have any margin of error. Our lives are so busy, so jam-packed, that we're tired, worn out, burned out, and yes, we are anxious. He suggests scheduling 80 percent of your life and leaving 20 percent unplanned—open for life to happen.

Feel better already? I hope so. Take whatever time you need to increase your health and energy level. Life requires training; dealing with difficult people uses energy you may not have. Pump up your body and mind and watch the road rage subside. To alleviate stress even further, go on to the next chapter, which will help you add fun to your to-do list and learn how and when it's still safe to have fun at work.

YOUR RELATIONSHIP TOOLBOX

HOW TO MOVE FROM PISSED OFF TO POWERFUL

PISSED OFF	POWERFUL
Working too much	Keeping your work life in balance
Neglecting your health because of work	Taking impeccable care of your body and mind
Missing sleep because of work or work worries	Sleeping eight to ten hours each night
Fueling your work with coffee and doughnuts	A healthful diet
Allowing others to decide how much you work	Setting healthy limits on work

12.
FUN IS NOT A FOUR LETTER WORD . . .
BUT WORK IS

How to stay sane and happy on the job.

Twice a day, at 11:00 A.M. and 5:00 P.M., a flock of ducks marches on red carpet in formation to the fountain at the Peabody Hotel in Memphis, Tennessee. The waddling ducks plop into the pool right on cue to the adoring applause of guests and staff. Twice a day, work stops and all the employees gather around to watch the ducks. Don't you wish that your workplace had a similar way to relax? Perhaps what makes your coworkers so difficult is that you have no way to have fun together. In this chapter, we'll look at ways that you might be able to lighten everyone up. One reason work is so stressful is that we've forgotten this essential tool.

Is There Any Fun to Be Had in a Politically Correct World?

Everyone in my office is just so sensitive these days!
Man, we can't have fun at work any more!
Why is everyone so PC around my company?

Sometimes, the difficult person in your work group may be someone you see as just too sensitive. As someone who's spent years in the trenches doing diversity and harassment training, I'm quite familiar with these PC complaints. Just how true are they? Well, I have to admit that there's a certain truth to them, driven by paranoia much more than reality. People these days are afraid to say or do things that *might* "offend" someone. This, as I frequently lament, rests on a total misunderstanding of the law and policy in this arena.

We do not have to worry about what might offend someone. In fact, if we did that, we wouldn't get any work accomplished, because we would be spending all our time trying to determine who or what might be offensive. That time is better spent learning what the law actually says and how our organization's policy reads. As outlined in Chapter 3, I can guarantee you that no matter what your location or company, the rules don't prohibit any remark that could possibly offend anyone.

There are millions of things we can still laugh and joke about at work and in fact, one of my core beliefs is that life is too short not to have fun at work! I say, go for it. Just don't make jokes about these twelve hot-button subjects:

- Race
- Sex
- Ethnic background
- Military status
- Disabilities
- Age
- Gender
- Sexual orientation
- Pregnancy
- National origin
- Religion

That's it! Now, that wasn't so hard, was it? Sometimes if I'm working with groups determined to gripe about these things, I force them to list all the things that are *okay* to joke about. The list includes subjects such as nerds, attorneys, sports teams, politicians, celebrities, the branch office, and the incompetence of headquarters. It may require more creativity to use appropriate humor. Talk to your kids. My experience is that they know great knock-knock jokes, jokes about Shrek, and on and on.

It can also be a lot of fun to get to know your colleagues on a deeper level. Contrary to popular belief, you can talk about where people grew up, the meaning of their last names, and the baby-to-be; you just can't do it in a derogatory or invasive way. How to make sure that you're not invading anyone's privacy or space? Offer similar information about yourself first. If you still have doubts about whether your inquires are welcome, *ask*. Ask people how they want to be treated; don't assume that they want to be treated the same way you do.

The Platinum Rule

In Western culture, most of us are familiar with the golden rule: Do unto others as you would have them do unto you. We tweak that a bit for the platinum rule: Treat others as *they would like to be treated*. Of course, this is extra effort, but in a diverse work world, nothing less will do. Let me suggest a few ideas for getting to know people so that you know them well enough to have fun. If you're having fun with someone, you're much less likely to perceive them as difficult!

If you see two people who are friends or close work colleagues, you can always ask them how they met. You could also offer them some of your own background or history. If we strive to be straightforward with others, it gives them permission to be straightforward with us.

One way to do this is to share a popular exercise we conduct in our diversity trainings: "cultural stories." We ask participants to remember a time when they felt different in some way from the dominant culture, a time when they experienced being an outsider.

For example, I frequently share that my first job out of law school was in Denver with a couple of attorneys who were born and raised in New York City. This was also their first job out of law school and their first time living outside of New York. As people do when they're getting to know each other, we were sharing our experiences growing up and I talked about how I had grown up in western Colorado on the rim of the Black Canyon on a sheep ranch. Not exactly the end of the world—but you can see it from there.

I shared with my New York colleagues how in the summers, we would herd the sheep on horseback from our summer permits up above Lake City. This was so strange to them that they thought I was joking and/or making this up. They could not believe that anyone still did that. They thought it was something that was reserved for the stuff of western movies, and more of a myth than a reality in this day and age. In fact, I worked with these two guys for two years and they never believed me. They joked about my being a cowgirl, told sheep jokes and, in general, thought I was a big spoofer.

I finally gave up trying to convince them and just let them believe that I was joking around. It was one of the first times in my life that I realized that the way I grew up was so different from others, people literally refused to believe it.

When we share these stories in our diversity training, we pair people off and then have one person share an experience of a time he or she felt other people didn't believe him or her. The partner repeats the story back to the first sharer and is graded on listening. The listener then shares his or her story while the first sharer listens and then repeats what they think they heard.

Using Humor to Connect with Difficult People

Sharing a joke with someone can lead to more connection and make them feel less difficult. Try the Good Clean Funnies List at *www.gcfl.net* when you're really stuck. You can get a free subscription to receive a "funny" a day, and you can even rate each joke. All jokes offered are in the public domain, so you're free to pass them along. What workplace couldn't use a dose of good clean fun? Humor also helps you to build rapport with your colleagues so that when issues do come up, you have a common ground of understanding.

HELP TAKE A LOAD OFF

If you're not having fun at work, it's easy to feel pissed off at everyone and everything. Perhaps instead, you could appoint yourself the fun master of your work group. My client Southwest Airlines, for example, built its brand by making the travel experience fun for customers and staff. Flight attendants pop out of overhead bins, joke on the announcements, and engage in other madcap antics.

LIGHTEN UP: SMILING IS PART OF THE DRESS CODE

Still having a problem having fun at work? Consider forcing yourself to smile. Yes, it's a scientific fact: smiling not only works the facial muscles but tricks our happiness hormones into thinking that they're doing better than they are. We can literally fake it until we make it.

Or, if you're really bold, start a laughing club at work. Seriously. Doctor Madan Kataria, a physician from Mumbai, India, is the founder of and chief proselytizer for Laughter Yoga, a movement that since 1995 has spawned 5,000 laughter clubs—in which people meet regularly just to laugh—worldwide. To date there are just 200 or so clubs in the United States, including those in Atlanta; New York; Orlando, Florida; St. Louis; and Tucson, Arizona. But Kataria hopes to change that over the next few years by training more teachers. (To learn more, go to *www.laughteryoga.org.*) "Our objective is to build an international community of people who believe in love and laughter" Kataria is quoted in *Yoga Journal.*

Most of the time is spent on what Kataria calls his "breakthrough technology": exercises designed to get people to laugh for no apparent reason. These, combined with simple yoga breathing techniques and "laughter meditation," are the heart of Laughter Yoga. Though little clinical research has been done to date, Kataria promises that Laughter Yoga relieves stress, boosts immunity, fights depression, and eventually transforms people into more positive thinkers.

Kataria explains why laughter is good for the body. "When you start laughing, your chemistry changes, your physiology changes, your chances to experience happiness are much greater," he says. "Laughter Yoga is nothing more than prepping the body and mind for happiness."

Kataria goes on to claim that laughter has two sources: one from the body and one from the mind. Adults, he believes, tend to laugh from the mind. "We make judgments and evaluations about what's funny and what isn't," he says. Children, who laugh much more frequently than adults, laugh from the body. "They laugh all the time they're playing. Laughter Yoga is based on cultivating your childlike playfulness. We all have a child inside us wanting to laugh, wanting to play." His theory is that we can relearn what we knew as children, laughing from the body rather than the brain.

The idea that laughter heals is not new. Norman Cousins, editor of the *Saturday Review*, documented his own laughter cure in the 1979 book *Anatomy of an Illness as Perceived by the Patient*. Cousins had been diagnosed in the mid-1960s with ankylosing spondylitis, a painful degenerative disease of the connective tissue that left him weak and barely able to move. Doctors gave him a 500-to-1 chance of recovery. Rejecting conventional treatments, Cousins checked out of the hospital and into a hotel, where he set up a film projector and played funny movies. He took massive doses of vitamin C and immersed himself in hours of the Marx Brothers. "I made the joyous discovery that ten minutes of genuine belly laughter had an anesthetic effect," he wrote, "and would give me at least two hours of pain-free sleep." Cousins recovered and lived for another twenty-six years. And, in part inspired by his experience, a handful of scientists began researching the healing power of laughter.

One of them was William Fry, then a psychiatrist at Stanford University. In a series of studies during a career that spanned more than fifty years, Fry documented some of the health benefits of what he calls "mirthful laughter." He found that laughter increases circulation, stimulates the immune system, exercises the muscles, and even invigorates the brain. Other researchers have found that laughter reduces stress hormones and may help prevent heart disease. Not to mention that laughter burns calories; how great is that?

I know you're wondering whether fake laughter—laughter devoid of humor, laughter that's forced rather than spontaneous—can have the same beneficial effects. Fry believes that aside from the mental stimulation that comes in the moment of discovery when you hear a good joke or appreciate a pun, the physical and emotional effects should be largely the same. "I think it's beneficial," says Fry, who has heard about but hasn't experienced Laughter Yoga. "I'm in favor of this program."

If nothing else, all that laughter practice will drive the liars and tyrants and boors down the hall crazy! You may want to try Laughter Yoga just for that reason.

THE PROVEN PERKS OF HUMOR

You may believe that you'd be more happy at work if all the difficult people left, but is that really true? Do we really know what will make us happy?

Recently, psychologists such as Martin Seligman of the University of Pennsylvania and his colleagues have challenged the widely accepted view that people are stuck with a basic setting on their happiness thermostat. That old view held that effects of good or bad life events such as marriage, a raise, divorce, or disability will simply fade with time. But recent long-term studies have revealed that the happiness thermostat is more malleable.

One new study showing change in happiness levels followed thousands of Germans for seventeen years. A quarter of them changed significantly over that time in their basic level of satisfaction with life. Nearly a tenth of the German participants changed by three points or more on a ten-point scale.

One of the things that does seem to show promise in creating more happiness is something so simple you may be inclined to dismiss it as moronic. Before going to sleep at night, think of three good things that happened that day and analyze why they occurred. "Once they start, people keep doing these things on their own because it's immediately rewarding," says Seligman colleague Acacia Parks. "Although this technique sounds Pollyanaish, you'll find yourself focusing more on good things that happen, which might otherwise be forgotten because of daily disappointments," she says.

A second approach that has shown promise in Seligman's group has people discover their personal strengths through a specialized questionnaire, and then choose the five most prominent ones. Every day for a week, each person is to apply one or more of his or her strengths in a new way—things like the ability to find humor or summon enthusiasm; appreciation of beauty; curiosity and love of learning. The exercise may be a good way to get engaged in satisfying activities, pumping up your general level of satisfaction, especially at work. For more ideas about raising your own happiness thermostat at work, read Seligman's book *Authentic Happiness.*

Why do I keep harping on encouraging you to increase your own level of happiness at work? Partly because fun is *fun*, but also because of a concept psychologists call "projection." We tend to project our internal feelings onto those around us, especially people with whom we're in conflict. Raising our own happiness set point helps lower our reactivity to those difficult people with whom we work. Moreover, it may cause the difficult person to feel happier or calmer, thus changing how he or she interacts with us. In the next chapter, you'll find even more ideas on how to smooth out difficult interactions.

YOUR
RELATIONSHIP TOOLBOX

HOW TO MOVE FROM PISSED OFF TO POWERFUL	
PISSED OFF	POWERFUL
Taking work too seriously	Looking for ways to have fun at work
Making fun of people's gender or ethnic background	Using appropriate humor to lighten up the workplace
Underestimating the power of laughter	Laughing more

13.
BE CHARMING EVEN IF IT KILLS YOU

How to adjust and harness your own attitude.

Laurie Frank's seventeen male colleagues huddle around the table in the wood-paneled conference room. Alternating between barbed snapping and backslapping, they trade golf scores, quarrel about the year-end financial statements, and trade opinions on which associates will make the cut. Laurie takes it all in with a knowing smile. After five years as a partner in this litigation-oriented law firm, she has learned a hard-won secret of survival: Be charming if it kills you. When asked how she manages in this cutthroat male bastion, she repeats her mantra and soldiers on. That wasn't always the case. There was a time when she used to sling punches and insults with the best of them; she fought fire with fire, sparking her share of flameouts. Laurie has realized that her maddening mother was right: You do attract more flies with honey than with vinegar.

The author of the book *Choosing Civility*, P.M. Forni of the Johns Hopkins Civility Project, argues that the habit of civility has a dual purpose: making others feel at ease in the world, and making yourself feel at ease in the world by holding yourself to high standards. If you cultivate your own civility, exercise emotional competence, place firm boundaries on your behavior, and refuse to allow others to strip you of your dignity and composure, you gain power and confidence that simply can't be matched by collecting snippy one-liners and insults.

You may never improve another's behavior by your own example, Forni believes, but you can always carry with you your own "shelter from life's slings and arrows": a firm determination to preserve your best self and walk away from altercations with your head high.

Why Yelling Doesn't Work

No question, we live in an uncivil age, which contributes to many workplace woes. We have a popular culture that tends to value in-your-face attitude: rappers, punk rockers, media shouting debates, racists and sexist movies, and porno Web sites. In the workplace, however, most organizations are moving in the opposite direction, enforcing stricter policies on harassment, discrimination, threats, and violence. Employers are realizing that they have a legal and ethical obligation to create a workplace that's safe and comfortable for everyone. They're also realizing that it makes good business sense because it helps attract and retain the best employees.

Many people come into the workplace, however, thinking that the loose atmosphere they encounter in other settings will work in the office. Not true. Many people, for example, may have risen to the top by using abusive language, and yelling and attacking the people who work for them. These leaders may have been seen as hard-charging and results-driven. They may have even succeeded in some settings. For example, Bobby Knight, the winningest coach in basketball history, was famous for this style.

However, such tactics—while they may succeed in the short run—ultimately fail, as they did for Knight. He was eventually fired from his high-profile job at Indiana University, spent a year unemployed, and finally found a place at the much less prestigious Texas Tech, where he's continued to create controversy there for some of his antics.

Theoretically, if you're abusive to everyone, it's not discrimination or harassment. I call such people "equal opportunity abusers." In today's work environment, however, even if you do yell, scream, and verbally attack everyone equally, eventually someone will come along who is different from you. That person may believe that you're abusing him or her *because* they're different. Then you have a serious issue on your hands.

When that person files a complaint against you for harassment or discrimination, how will you defend yourself? By arguing that you do this to everyone? How will you prove that fact? You'll have to call all the people you've abused to come and testify that "yup, he did it to me too!" What will the judge or jury think of you at that point? That you're a jerk, of course. Trust me, the outcome will not be in your favor.

Beyond the law, there are other good reasons to practice civility. Ultimately, it works better than anything else. I loved watching the commentary on Indianapolis Colts coach Tony Dungy after his Super Bowl victory. Apparently, when he took over as coach, he called his team in and announced in a soft voice, "This is the loudest you'll ever hear me talk, so you better listen well." Even during the Super Bowl game, he never appeared to lose his cool, and reporters who were in the locker room afterward talked about the great respect each player had for Dungy. They wanted to play hard and win because of their boundless admiration for him.

Setting high expectations for courtesy and civility with staff, clients, bosses, and colleagues will always serve you. Model respectful behavior yourself. Create policies around it if you're a leader in your organization, and be sure you walk the talk. Don't tolerate abusive behavior from others, and don't engage in abuse.

As a seminar leader, I always bend over backward to treat my audience with extreme politeness and respect, even when we're dealing with hot issues and they lose their cool. Ultimately, it always pays off. As a participant in one of my seminars said, "I do a lot of training and I've never thought of politeness as a technique, but I noticed that you used it and I'm going to try it myself."

Sometimes that's not easy. One time, for example, I was dealing with a group of orthopedic surgeons who had been sued for harassing nurses in the operating room, were continuing to deal with high staff turnover because of their disrespectful behavior, and were at each others' throats every day. As the session became more heated, the most severely abusive doctor became so frustrated with me that he started yelling about how they were surgeons, their jobs were stressful, and that this was "not a @#$% charm school!"

He kept escalating his rude remarks. I responded firmly and politely. He finally became so enraged that he stomped out of the session. Calmly, I continued on without him.

Later that night, he called me at my hotel to apologize for his behavior. Since we were in a western state and I knew he'd understand what I meant, I just replied cheerily, "Oh that's all right. Don't worry. It's not my first rodeo."

"I suspected that it was not," he replied, clearly chagrined.

The next day, he returned to the meeting and behaved like a model student.

While it can be difficult to practice in the moment, charm wins in the long run. You should never be a doormat, and you should clearly know and enforce your own limits, but you can always do so in a civil way. Let me give you some examples of what I mean.

SPECIFIC TACTICS FOR RUDE BEHAVIOR	
BEHAVIOR	**CIVIL RESPONSE**
Yelling and screaming	Calmly saying, "I need you to speak in a normal voice. I can't listen when you yell."
Profanity	"I'm sure you didn't mean to say that, but profanity really doesn't work for me. Please choose other language."
Stomping out	Calling or meeting later and saying, "I know you were upset, and I'm glad that you took a time-out, but can we talk in a productive way now?"
Interrupting/talking over you	"I know you have a lot of ideas and I appreciate your passion but I can't keep track of the conversations if you keep interrupting me. Please stop."
Condescending tone	"I'm sure that you didn't intend that the way it sounded but I felt really diminished when you said what you did. I need you to respect my experience and expertise and how hard I've been working to figure this out. Please try to talk to me in a kind way."

Of course, some people just behave this way on a regular basis, and you may need to constantly remind them of your limits. Using the 1-2-3-Go! technique of making requests for different behavior in Chapter 6 will also help set limits with someone who refuses to respect you. If all of your attempts fail, of course, you'll have to appeal to a higher authority, as outlined in Chapter 16.

In your interactions with the misbehaving person, as well as your manager or HR when and if you have to complain, keep in mind one important rule: You do have the right to be treated with respect at work. This is true even if you've made a mistake or done something wrong. You can, and should, correct any errors and apologize when you mess up, but you need to remember your limits: you don't give abuse and you don't tolerate it from others.

YOUR RELATIONSHIP TOOLBOX

HOW TO MOVE FROM PISSED OFF TO POWERFUL	
PISSED OFF	POWERFUL
Fighting fire with fire	Remaining civil, even when others are not
Yelling, screaming, profanity	Using strong, dignified language
Tolerating abuse	Setting clear boundaries against bad treatment
Bad manners	Civility

14.
HOW TO SHINE AT ANY JOB AND WHY YOU SHOULD

Great expectations.

After he returned from serving in the Marines in Vietnam, Bill started out working as a pizza delivery person. Bill was a college dropout, and the words of his MD/JD father rang in his ears as he made his deliveries: "You never finished college! You're just a screwup!" Still, Bill liked working. He was good with people, a natural salesperson, a quick study, and attentive to details. Bill's manager quickly promoted him to assistant manager. When that manager left, Bill took over as manager. His store's sales climbed. Next thing he knew, he was managing nine pizza stores. He attracted the attention of the head of a major hotel chain, who hired him to help run the front desk of one of his hotels. Soon, Bill was managing that hotel and steadily working his way up the promotion ladder. He recently retired after serving as the senior vice president of operations. The secret of his success? Doing his very best every day at every job.

The Value of Doing Your Current Job Well

If you're going to be a street sweeper, to paraphrase Dr. Martin Luther King Jr., be the Michelangelo of Street Sweepers. King preached in the value of the dignity of all work. You may not like your job now, but there's always value in doing a good job, even if you're surfing Monster.com looking for a better alternative.

Consider the life story of Chris Gardner, played by Will Smith in the movie *The Pursuit of Happyness*. Gardner took an unpaid internship at the bottom of the heap in a Wall Street brokerage firm. As the first black salesperson at the firm, he had a lot to prove. While living on the street with his young son, he worked hard every day and overcame tremendous obstacles, eventually becoming one of the firm's top producers. The message he preaches in the motivational speeches he gives today is simple: Do your best wherever you are.

At this point you may be snarling, "What does all this motivational talk have to do with people pissing you off at work?" Everything! It's darn near impossible not to snap at the kook in the next cube if you hate every minute of your job and feel that what you do doesn't matter.

There Are No Small Parts, Only Small Actors

Do you think that every person who reached great heights started out at the top or worked with easy coworkers? Consider Leonardo Da Vinci, one of the leading figures of the Renaissance. Besides his abilities as a painter, he was a superb draftsman, sculptor, architect, engineer, and writer. His notebooks are filled with scientific musings and mechanical inventions that were centuries ahead of their time. "Knowing how to see" was his mantra. He wrote that he spent his days trying hard to see whatever was in front of him, instead of worrying about the next artistic commission.

Da Vinci's first job at age fifteen was as an apprentice to the artist Andrea del Verrocchio, a notorious, temper-tantrum-throwing prima donna. Despite his formidable talent, Da Vinci was relegated to mixing paints. How did Da Vinci rise to such heights despite such menial work? Perhaps it was his focus on seeing the opportunities (however humble) that were right in front of him, instead of complaining about those that were not there.

Doing Your Job Impeccably Will Always Serve You

Can all jobs have dignity and meaning? Yes, I believe they can. If you don't believe me, review Viktor Frankl's book, *Man's Search for Meaning*, in which he talks about his time as a prisoner in a concentration camp. His "job" was caring for the bodies after the victims had been gassed or otherwise executed. Sometimes the dead piled up in great heaps; an unimaginable, horrible sight! Yet, Frankel approached his duties with dignity and care, lovingly attending to each body as a religious act. He knew the one great truth: Our oppressors can take away everything from us except our own freedom of thought and our dignity.

The Dalai Lama tells a similar story about a Tibetan monk who was jailed and tortured by the Chinese for many years after they took over Tibet. When asked if he was ever frightened, the monk replied: "Yes, one time. I was in danger of losing my compassion for the Chinese."

Now, of course, we can't all expect to carry the enlightenment and equanimity of a Tibetan monk or Viktor Frankl, but we can treat our own work as something important, and even sacred, if we have that kind of spiritual orientation. There are few things more motivating than viewing our daily rounds as a kind of service to something higher and greater than our own lives.

As Rhonda Britten, author of *Fearless Living*, puts it: "Complaining only exacerbates the problem by focusing your attention on what is wrong in your life rather than focusing on taking actions to solve it or accepting the situation as is and finding peace with it."

Complaining drains our energy. If we can see our work—no matter how lowly—in a larger context, that will always serve us. One way to do that is to simply focus on each day as an act of service, as Martin Luther King Jr. stressed.

If you want to shine at your job—and be happier in the process—look for ways in which your being there serves others. For example, you may be a humble assistant, but what if your smile and pleasant "good morning" is what brightens up a dismal colleague's day? Look for small ways to serve in any position you are in.

Finding Meaning in the Mundane

What's the real way to make work meaningful? By having a larger purpose that's big enough and wide enough to encompass your life at work or at home. For example, my larger purpose is always to build relationships and to lessen the distance between people. That always helps me to stay "on purpose" wherever I am and guides all that I do and say. Even though I get as tired and cranky as everyone else, having a purpose helps motivate me to keep on trucking on my worst days.

Similarly, writer and long-time Zen Buddhist practitioner Natalie Goldberg, in her writing about her teacher, Katagiri

Roshi, in the book *The Great Failure: A Bartender, a Monk, and My Unlikely Path to Truth,* details the challenge of rising every day at 4:00 A.M. to sit still and meditate in the Zendo. Yet rise and sit Goldberg did—all through her thirties she sat still. As Goldberg puts it: "an age when others were investing their energy in building careers, a vast opportunity was presented to me—to meet my own mind and 'to have kind consideration for all sentient beings every moment forever.'" That larger purpose kept Goldberg going.

Nat sat on, guided by Roshi's three great teachings:

- Continue under all circumstances
- Don't be tossed away—don't let anything stop you
- Make positive effort for the good

Whatever your spiritual orientation, these are principles that you can apply to your work situation.

Practical Tips to Stay On Purpose in Any Job

The reality of most jobs is that you *do* have to deal with difficult coworkers, bosses, clients, and customers, and you may not receive the tangible things you want in every job—the big title, big money, prestige, location, and fulfillment. You can, however, embrace and live your higher purpose in any job, even while you may be searching for the next one.

You may also be able to develop tangible rewards even from a job you hate: contacts, learning new skills, and/or learning what you don't want to do and being grateful for a better job when one does show up.

Think a moment about what your higher purpose is. Whatever it is, it has to give you enough perspective that you don't worry about whatever the bozos are doing on a daily basis, because you know in your heart that you're doing what you came to earth to do and that what you do on a daily basis *matters*.

FINDING YOUR HIGHER PURPOSE

Perhaps you don't know what your higher purpose is right now. Well, for today, just do what's in front of you. If like Michelangelo you're mixing paints, do it with zeal; if like Bill you're delivering pizza, do it with style. You never know where such focus might lead you—perhaps to a prestigious art commission or to a top position in a major hotel chain.

One way to decide what your purpose might be is to imagine a deathbed scene: Yours. No, it doesn't have to be a macabre one; you may—since you're writing this scene—imagine one full of peace with your family and friends all around you. What memories are you all laughing (or crying) about? What scenes do you remember fondly from your long life? What are you most proud of accomplishing? What will others miss about not having you on the planet? Any regrets? Anyone you need to forgive or ask forgiveness from? What did you leave unfinished? Do you care about what's in your inbox or on your endless to-do list? What flowers sit in the vase by your bed? What music serenades you into your transition?

Take as long as you like to imagine the best possible ending. Yes, there is such a thing as a good death. When you're finished, write down all the details and then put it away for at least a couple of days, and preferably a couple of weeks.

After your scene has had time to "mulch," take your writing out and read through the passage again as if you were reading about someone else. What would you say about the person who lies dying in this scene? What was his or her purpose on earth? Did that person accomplish what he or she came to earth to do? And most important, what can you do today to make sure that you do accomplish your purpose?

You Just Need to Keep Working No Matter What

Sam Moore popularized the song "Soul Man" long before the Blues Brothers decided to cover it. Terry Gross, host of the NPR program *Fresh Air*, recently asked Moore if he ever fought boredom as he sang his most famous song over and over. "Absolutely" he replied. "But sometimes you just got to shut up and get up there and do it anyway."

Nothing could be truer than that. Bored with your job? Annoyed to tears by your lying, boring, screaming coworkers? Shut up and get up there and do it anyway.

You're probably asking, "How do you put up and shut up when your boss, clients, and coworkers are making you want to give up the will to live?" Try a perspective check. Think your job is bad? On a really bad day go to the Discovery Channel on TV or online and check out the popular Mike Rowe show *Dirty Jobs*. Every week Mike works for a day with some of the "unsung American laborers who make their living in the most unthinkable—yet vital—ways."

Consider the lot of penguin cage cleaner, sewer inspector, oyster shucker, sludge cleaner, or mosquito control officer, for example, if you think your job sucks. One of my favorite of Mike's picks is the occupation of chicken sexer. Yes, it's just what you think. Workers line up every day to determine whether chicks are boys or girls before sending them to their very different fates. It does give one perspective on our own worst days, doesn't it?

In the next chapter, you may find some ideas to help you stay on purpose. You'll learn about focus and intensity—two critical factors for fulfilling any purpose at work.

YOUR
RELATIONSHIP TOOLBOX

HOW TO MOVE FROM PISSED OFF TO POWERFUL	
PISSED OFF	POWERFUL
Hating your job	Finding a way to give any job meaning
Doing poor work	Doing your best, no matter what your job
Believing purpose doesn't matter	Discovering your purpose
Being in a meaningless daze	Purposely being

15.
TAKE THIS JOB AND LOVE IT

How to enjoy everything at work.

Sarah Jones stares out the window of her office, fantasizing about possessing X-Men superpowers. If she were Angel, she'd unfold her wings and fly to freedom. If she were Wolverine, she'd pop out her six-inch claws and get the idiot in accounting who'd ruined her day. If she were Storm, she'd use her weather power to zap her boss with a lighting bolt for giving her such a lousy bonus. No such luck. With a huge sigh and a scowl, she returns to piling and unpiling the stacks of undone work on her desk, haunted by dreams of improbable rescue.

Get Intense: Work with More Energy and Focus

One of the classic works on mood is David D. Burns's *Feeling Good*. This popular work on cognitive therapy posits that, when we're feeling down, almost any activity makes us feel better. Even more surprising, we're lousy at predicting which tasks will make us feel better or worse.

STOP Pissing Me Off!

Burns suggested that his patients keep logs of various activities and how they felt before and after performing each activity. One woman planned many activities that she anticipated would make her feel better. What was the one that actually resulted in the biggest mood boost? Balancing her checkbook! Like most of us, she dreaded this task but had found that once she started, she focused on the satisfaction of getting it done.

As you learned in earlier chapters, you are not a helpless victim of your mood. Exercise, healthy sleep patterns, diet, and appropriate expression of our emotions all play a role in our mood and energy level. If we're unable to lift our mood with these measures, we need to seek medical help and/or therapy.

Working with energy, concentration, and focus is its own reward. Study after study has shown that working at this level actually raises levels of dopamine, one of the "feel-good" neurotransmitters, in your brain. Clearly, you need high energy and a good mood to work with difficult people.

Trying to boost your mood, however, can be a Catch-22. You have low dopamine because of health issues, your attitude toward work, or the crank down the hall; so, you don't feel like working. The more you avoid working with energy and focus, the more your brain chemistry plunges—and then everyone and everything annoys you. The problem becomes a self-fulfilling prophecy.

What is needed here is a dose of good old-fashioned faith and will. You have to believe that you will feel better when you engage in the work rather than avoid it, and then you must will yourself to do it. Your work, of course, includes using all the skills in this book to learn how to manage difficult people.

One way to pull this off is to follow Burns's cognitive recipe. It involves identifying the thoughts underneath your feelings. If you feel sad, depressed, and uninspired, for example, what thoughts (or cognitive distortions, as Burns calls them) might be underlying these feelings?

In Sarah's case, those thoughts might be "globalization," the belief that the nut in accounting will *always* behave in an annoying way and that her boss will *never* give her a decent bonus. If she looks under her mood to these thoughts and talks back to them, she discovers that—even though her bonus last year was disappointing—the year before that she'd received a bonus that was more than she'd expected. Similarly, although Patrick in accounting could be a jerk, he had helped her out on end-of-quarter deadlines more often than she could count.

Other cognitive distortions include black-and-white thinking (for example, people are all good or all bad), mind reading (I know my blind date hates my blue skirt), catastrophizing (no matter what project I take on, I'll fail). If you learn to talk back to your mood when it's founded on such unrealistic thoughts, you can sometimes pull yourself out of a funk.

WHEN TO SEEK HELP

If these "at home" remedies don't work, you may need to decide whether you're clinically depressed. If you are, you'll find it nearly impossible to manage difficult people at work. How to tell? The American Psychological Association (*www.apa.org*) offers this test in order to tell the difference between the blues—or occasional mild depression—and a major depressive disorder. The difference is one of frequency. The following symptoms are possible signs of clinical depression:

- Persistent sadness
- Diminished interest in your favorite activities
- Difficulty concentrating

- Loss of appetite—or increased appetite
- Trouble sleeping—or sleeping too much
- Feeling restless or agitated
- Feeling worthless
- Recurrent thoughts of death or suicide

If your symptoms interfere with your everyday life, if you find that you're canceling all social plans, or you keep missing work because you can't get out of bed, talk to a mental-health specialist.

Be aware also that the most recent research finds a definite link between physical pain and brain chemistry problems such as bipolar disorder or depression. This doesn't mean that it's "all in your head," but simply that the neurotransmitters in the brain that govern physical pain are, in some way that we don't totally understand, connected to those that govern mood. Treatment for these mood disorders can sometimes help solve physical problems as well.

Work Is Easier with Energy and Focus

The truth is that 95 percent of what we do in a day is a bitch. We don't want to get up at 5:00 A.M. to go the gym, we don't want to work on a particular project, or deal with certain people, and so on. However, you'll feel much better if you're totally committed and engaged in what you're doing in the moment—even if it's not exactly what you want to be doing. You may make a decision to do something different tomorrow or next week, but today, if you can work with 100 percent commitment, that level of engagement will turn out to be its own reward.

If you doubt this, read the research of Mihaly Csikszentmihaly. In his classic work *Flow: The Psychology of Optimal Experience*, he tracked ordinary people to find out what put them into the state that winning athletes and creative artists reach when they're performing at their peak, totally engaged in the moment, and "flowing" without effort or strain. What he found was that ordinary individuals also achieve this state, frequently without knowing how they managed to do so. What worked, in part, was that they dove into what they were doing with 100 percent commitment, even when they didn't feel like it.

Essentially, Csikszentmihaly contends that most people are not happy because the universe wasn't created to make them happy; on the contrary, life and the universe serves to frustrate us and help us grow. Yet "flow" states happen to people despite the challenges of the universe, and they happen to people from all walks of life, from all cultures, throughout the world.

People who are in "flow" achieve a state of consciousness that's in harmony with their surroundings and feelings. They don't make distinctions between work and play; they create an inner state of being that brings them peace and fulfillment that's separate from their external environment. They're focused and feel that what they do is meaningful and has purpose. They're absorbed in their activities, with a sense of connection to their inner self and also with others. The flow state helps create enjoyment and satisfaction with one's quality of life, including work. Some people experience flow for minutes, some for hours, some for days on end.

While the faith that we can move into flow can be difficult to muster when the annoying boss or colleague takes us to task, the latest psychological research shows that motivation follows action not the other way around, as we may believe.

You may be wondering, "What does all of this have to do with working with the jerk down the hall? I'm supposed to be learning how to work with difficult people, not how to change my own mood." The thing is, if you let your curmudgeonly colleagues determine how happy you are, you are setting yourself up for failure. Life is unfair and there will always be a jerk somewhere. Will that person bring you down? Bet money on it. However, by knowing how to manage your mood you can love (or at least like) being wherever you are even if your boss is a brute, your coworkers are awful, and the job or organization is hellish.

Before you abandon your current job, however, I'd urge you to consider that you might be able to use more of your strengths and therefore work happier by tweaking your work just a bit. As Marcus Buckingham points out in *Putting Your Strengths to Work*, most people feel drained by too many activities at work that don't use their strengths, but they could still find a good fit in their current position. What it takes is to discover your strengths and do more of those activities, while doing less of the activities that play to your weakness and drain you. In addition to self-analysis, of course, you also need to learn how to communicate with your boss and coworkers so they'll support your efforts.

Beat the Flow-Busters

One of the reasons we don't reach that flow state is that we all suffer from modern life-induced ADD. In order to have more flow and less ADD, try the following tips:

Ignore e-mail. I know this is heresy in our e-mail–obsessed culture but trust me, the "e" in e-mail stands for "endless." It will be there and you will be able to check it later. I tell all my clients and associates that I only check e-mail twice a day and that if it's an emergency (someone had better be bleeding), the best way to reach me is by phone. Turn off the sound that alerts you to every incoming message and take a deep breath. You can do it. Most messages are not that important. If it's your boss demanding attention, train him to wait. Trust me, he's trainable. Try using, for example, the 1-2-3-Go! technique outlined earlier in this book.

Phone less. Don't pick up the phone on each ring. Let calls accumulate and then return phone calls twice a day, perhaps as near to 9:00 A.M. and 5:00 P.M. as you can. At these hours, people are apt to be in but not as busy as other times. And use your outgoing message strategically: Ask people to leave their number first so you don't have to listen to endless rumbling.

Gossip on schedule. While gossip can serve as the invisible glue that binds us to our coworkers and helps make work more fun, it can also be a huge time-sucker. Don't let people just drop by. Schedule trips to the coffeepot and block off fifteen-minute slots for visiting. If you have an office, close the door and hang up a sign. (Remember Lucy in the "Peanuts" cartoon? The doctor is "In" or not.) If you work in a cube, find a cute sign to put up or wear a hat that makes it clear you're unavailable. Consider red for "stop—don't bother me," and green for "okay, come on in."

One of our neighbors, the mother of three popular kids, despaired about the constant ringing phones and chiming doorbells. After a trip to Switzerland, the family landed on this system: Hanging up the Swiss flag meant that they were in a neutral state: not receiving visitors. No Swiss flag meant come on in! Even the smallest kids learned and respected the system. If kids can do it, your boss can also. As Dr. Phil loves to opine, we train people how to treat us.

Brain dump. Take fifteen minutes at the end of every day to conduct a "brain dump" and make a to-do list for tomorrow.

Clean off your desk so that you can walk in with a clear view the next day. When things get bad, I clean off my desk and put everything on the floor in front of it, where I can't see the piles. Not a great long-term solution, but for bad days, it's a lifesaver. I get a respite from all the depressing piles on my desk and the mental (and physical) space to tackle what I need to.

If these self-help strategies don't work, you may need to hire the help of a professional organizer, time-management expert, and/or psychiatrist for your scattered thinking. Call for help whenever the going gets rough. What's at stake is your very ability to enjoy your life. Work engages such a big chunk of your time that if you hate your work, you will be miserable for every hour you are there, and eventually that unhappiness will even bleed into non-work time.

As Aristotle observed, all humans seek happiness. This hasn't changed in thousands of years, but you may need to work harder to achieve that flow state than the ancient Greeks did. People today simply have too many choices, too much stuff, and too much to do. Unless you can pare down, you're unlikely to be happy, and everyone's likely to annoy you.

Deal Me In!

Though you should strive to pare down nonessential tasks, there are benefits of beneficence. That doesn't mean becoming a workaholic or committing to more than you can reasonably do. What it does mean is engaging in the work that really matters—such as helping colleagues. Unless your workload is crushing, you'll actually feel better, not worse, the more you agree to take on projects with other people. The feedback from working with them, and the joy it will bring you in terms of the helpful brain chemicals of connection (see Chapter 4) will bring you necessary rewards.

The Dalai Lama and other popular Buddhist leaders have brought the world many blessings. One of them is what the Dalai Lama calls the "science of compassion." As a part of his work with the Mind and Life Institute (*www.mindandlife.org*), which is a periodic gathering of respected neuroscientists and Buddhist leaders, he has been able to confirm the scientific validity of a standard Buddhist teaching: We should cultivate kindness because it makes us feel good, not just because it blesses the world. At the level of our brain chemistry, we feel good when we help others (even those we don't like!).

Why Kindness Matters Even in Your Workplace

But, you may protest, I have no desire to extend beneficence or healing power to my worst workplace enemy! If you need an attitude adjustment, consider the thoughts of Holocaust survivor Elie Wiesel. "I believe you must respect human dignity," he said. "I have fought all my life for that. I do not believe that the end justifies the means." Wiesel stated that he himself saw men, women, and children sacrificed on an altar of racists and religious hatred. He nearly died at forced labor. Freed from Auschwitz as a teenager, he wandered Europe as an "undesirable." He settled in France, where he went to college and became a journalist—or, as he likes to say, "a witness." "Suffering confers no privileges," Wiesel states. As Wiesel paraphrased Nietzsche, "If you fight the devil, you become one." "Hate," Wiesel says, "is an infectious disease." If Wiesel can embrace beneficence and forgiveness after his experience in hell, surely we can survive our own workplace bullies and boors.

How to Use the Force to Control Your Own Anger

Though we know that angry outbursts in the workplace do more harm than good, we may need extra help and an attitude adjustment to control them. If you need more incentive to dial it back a notch, consider this: A new study in the *Annals of Family Medicine* estimates that about 10 percent of emergency room cases could be avoided if people didn't take action when they were angry. At three ERs in Missouri, injury patients who'd felt "irritable" before their accidents were 30 percent more likely to get hurt, while "hostile" people had double the injury risk of the normal, non-inquired population. Next time you want to slap a difficult coworker, keep your anger in check and try this one-minute exercise instead.

1. Sit in a chair with your feet on the floor and your eyes closed. Picture a stop sign and say to yourself, "Stop." Take three deep breaths, and as you exhale, say, "Relax."
2. Clench your fists while inhaling and relax them as you exhale. Clench your toes as you inhale and relax them while exhaling.
3. Shrug your shoulders while inhaling, and then relax them as you exhale.
4. Inhale while tilting your head to the right, then exhale as you straighten. Repeat to the left. Inhale, and then relax. Open your eyes and reorient yourself.

Adapted from *In Control: No More Snapping at Your Family, Sulking at Work, Steaming in the Grocery Line, Seething at Meetings, StuffingYour Frustration* by Redford Williams, MD, and Virginia Williams, PhD.

Changing Your Workplace Culture

If all your attempts to convince or cajole your workplace "problem children" to behave seem to fail, you can still take responsibility for dealing with your own piece of the puzzle. You always retain the power to take unilateral action. Most of the strategies we've discussed so far require a certain amount of willingness and cooperation on the part of your coworkers in order to change the organization. Sometimes, however, people may promise to change while dragging their heels on actually doing so. Even then, you have more power than you might expect. You can still incubate positive change. By modeling for others the changes you would like to see in them, you can be effective in increasing your influence on the organization and indeed changing your very workplace DNA.

For example, one of my clients, Bill, was a young vice president of a pharmaceutical corporation. The company had recently merged with a much larger organization, creating layers of bureaucracy that both Bill and his group resisted. At some point, Bill realized that his team's own actions were undermining its effectiveness, and he decided to persuade his team to abandon their protest. His words fell on deaf ears. They simply refused to budge. He tried again. They dug their heels in further. He circled back for another round. They shunned him. Finally, he briefly flirted with the idea of firing the entire lot. The momentary respite of that fantasy gave him the will to try something else, something more subtle. He stopped talking and just acted. Calmly, without a word, he just changed his own behavior and abandoned the notion of changing the group's approach.

Bill followed the rules the new ownership demanded. When appropriate, he continued to advise his team of his own decisions to "go with the flow." He dealt with his employees, as well as his supervisors, in a fair and even-handed manner, avoiding the politics and passive-aggressive sabotage that some of his teammates delivered. He stopped lecturing his group on how they needed to follow his example and surrender to the enemy. He remained a calm and cheerful example of leadership.

Gradually, his employees adjusted and followed his lead. Although they continued to insist that they liked the old regime better, they slowly adapted to the new ways. Their resistance melted in droplets, but it did melt away.

Today, Bill is an executive vice president and his team leads the organization in sales for their global conglomerate. While people sometimes still talk about the "good old days," they don't actively resist the efforts and directives of headquarters. In five years, it's likely that they'll end up referring to these times as the good old days, too!

While one individual may not be able to change a whole system, you can always control your own behavior within the system and whether or not you continue to work for the organization. This gives you power. When you give up fighting with the other combatants without expecting that they change, you inspire by example, instead of convincing by argument.

USE UNILATERAL ACTION

As you take on the role of leading in this way, it helps to tell your coworkers what you expect and then to be sure that you walk the talk. Use "I" statements and talk only about your own side of the street, instead of their bad behavior. Outline the ways in which you will change, instead of asking for others to change or focusing on their past misdeeds.

For your own sanity, give up hoping that others will appreciate your efforts. Someday they may, but in the meantime, if you're using unilateral action, you need to attend to your own business. If you do notice tiny changes in the direction you want others to move, appreciate their efforts, no matter how small.

Last, but certainly not least, spend some time thinking about why the system seems so resistant to change and what kinds of healthier systems you could encourage.

One of my clients, Diana, an HR manager who had a long-running battle with John, a marketing director, used this technique. John had continually ignored and even sabotaged various HR policies that he considered a waste of his time and energy. Diana, however, had to deal with an indignant parade of employees bullied by John's "take-no-prisoners" management style. She tried to persuade John that he was violating good management practices, as well as company policy. No matter what approach she tried, he rebuffed her efforts.

After talking with me, she devised a new plan. Trapped in a no-win game, Diana found John working late one night and informed him that she was no longer going to harangue him about the problems he was causing employees. She realized that he didn't want or seem to need her advice, and so she would stop the campaign. Diana told him that she would inform employees that John would be handling his own HR problems henceforth. (How do we like that for shrewd?) She explained her new policy without anger and advised John that she was open to suggestions about how they could make their relationship work better.

For once, Diana stunned John into silence. While initially not willing to acknowledge her efforts, he started to seek out Diana for advice and counsel over time, as employee complaints started piling up on his desk like planes stacked up for takeoff over O'Hare airport. Today, while Diana still ruefully describes John as one of her "problem children," the unilateral truce seems to be working.

While such unilateral disarmament may appear to demonstrate weakness during the throes of battle, it can actually lead to a more lasting peace than would continuing a futile fight.

History offers many examples of unilateral action-yielding results. In 1948, for example, several years after the end of World War II, Soviet leader Joseph Stalin blockaded West Berlin, insisting that Allied troops leave the city. The Western Allies considered blasting through the blockade with an armed convoy but feared starting World War III. Instead, they chose the unilateral action of mounting a huge airlift of food and supplies to the isolated Berliners. Frustrated, Stalin called off the blockade and agreed to negotiate.

Sometimes we can use skillful words to turn around a stalled situation. During the American Civil War, for example, President Lincoln spoke sympathetically about the Southern rebels in a public address. Fully aware that he would need to unify the country after the war, he started the process of healing with his own unilateral action. When a staunch Unionist lambasted him for speaking kindly of his enemies when he should be destroying them, Lincoln answered with his classic reply: "Why, madam, do I not destroy my enemies when I make them my friends?"

Sometimes you just have to "Walk On," as U2 reminds us. That's what schoolteacher Christine Pelton of Piper, Kansas, decided to do. After discovering that nearly a fifth of her biology students had plagiarized their semester projects from the Internet, Pelton sought and received the backing of the district to fail the twenty-eight sophomores. Yet after parents complained, the school board reversed the decision. Her integrity at stake, Pelton resigned when she couldn't convince the board to change its stance. "The students no longer listened to what I had to say," she said. "They knew if they didn't like anything in my classroom from here on out, they can just go to the school board and complain."

Pelton didn't feel that she could compromise her own honest standards if she stayed. In this case, the costs to her own personal integrity would have been too great. When conflict violates our own sense of self and what's most important to our identity, sometimes the best solution is to just "walk on."

When all of your other frantic efforts to deal with the liars, tyrants, and boors at work have failed, you may need to walk. You may decide to walk into the office of a higher authority or another job all together, the subjects of the last two chapters.

YOUR RELATIONSHIP TOOLBOX

HOW TO MOVE FROM PISSED OFF TO POWERFUL	
PISSED OFF	**POWERFUL**
Working without focus or energy	Doing what it takes to work with flow
Becoming less and less effective at work	Seeking help if you can't focus
Allowing others to interrupt your energy	Managing your time and interruptions
Disconnecting from coworkers	Compassion and connection
Exploding in anger	Managing your own moods
Allowing others to control conflict	Taking unilateral actions

16.
IF ALL ELSE FAILS,
PULL THE FIRE ALARM

How to get their attention.

Jed had a reputation as a "hands on," caring San Francisco Bay area CEO. He knew his entire staff of one-hundred employees well—in addition to their spouses and children. He'd built a successful construction business, and didn't hesitate to wade into the trenches with "his guys" and always leave his door open for questions or conversation.

After the dotcom bust, the business tanked. Projects stalled, clients paid late. His foreman and managers started bickering among themselves about who was doing the most work, what resources were available, and even more trivial concerns. "They're fighting about every nut and bolt that goes out of the warehouse," complained Jed. "I don't have time to mediate; I have my own problems."

Sometimes It Needs to Be All About You

If you've read this far I hope you've tried all the techniques to resolve your workforce dilemma: you've learned to identify when it's you, not them; you've learned to make requests, not complaints; and, you've managed your own stress and happiness level. And yet....the issue (and the difficult coworker) remains. This chapter contains some last ditch suggestions to solve the problem.

Recycling conflict—the kind that repeats itself and doesn't ever get fully resolved—creates many workplaces messes. Einstein once said, "Problems cannot be solved at the same level of consciousness that created them." That Einstein quotation holds a key to the successful resolution of recycling conflict. The problem is the human tendency to try to solve a conflict by doing *more* of what already isn't working. As Einstein also supposedly said, "Insanity is repeating the same behavior and expecting different results."

If, for example, two managers are locked in a conflict about the budget, they tend to repeat strategies that are not working. One person gets more logical, for example, while the other person gets more emotional. Both people are bent on being right about some issue. As the conflict heats up, both individuals argue more forcefully for the "rightness" of their position. Neither person realizes that it's the act of needing to be right that's causing the problem. If you tend to be one of the people who share this need to be right, ask yourself, "Would I rather be right or would I rather be happy?"

Beyond that question, when you notice you're locked in a repeated conflict with whatever workplace boor or tyrant is driving you batty, try to stop yourself and become conscious of the repetitive nature of the conflict. Add the crucial ingredient of awareness. Notice when you're stuck in the same conflict, and make a conscious choice to abandon a pattern with no positive payoff. When you catch yourself doing more of what already isn't working, pause and do something—anything!—else.

Having a "Good" Fight

Take a deep breath and dig down to a different level. Frequently, the way out of a recycling conflict is to fight more, not less! Yes, you read that statement correctly. If a conflict persists, it may be because you're not discussing the deeper issue. For example, as is frequently the case, Jed's underlings weren't fighting enough about the right issues. They actually needed to fight more! When I sat down with them, some basic detective work revealed that they were all incredibly worried about the financial health of the business but no one was talking about that issue. They were all too frightened. Jed—because of his own pressure and worries—was not talking about money either. In fact, his usual available self had gone missing. He'd withdrawn and spent more and more time in the office with the door closed, poring over the financials. His behavior scared everyone.

The solution? Jed needed to come clean. He needed to share the financial reality of the company with his employees and seek their input on how to make things work during the economic downturn. These discussions generated more fights and conflicts, but they created productive conflicts, what I call "good" fights. Conflict about ideas and about the right issues— not personality disputes or excuses to torpedo the other guy— lead to good fights.

Here are some questions and comments that will encourage your coworkers to cough up the real issues, not whatever they're fussing about on the surface. Once someone has stated his or her position (solution to the problem), try these responses:

- I'm wondering why you want X?
- When did you first decide that you wanted X?
- If you can't get X, what will you do?

- If you can't get X, what's the next best thing?
- What's important to you about X?
- What's most important to you about X?
- What's least important to you about X?
- I'm puzzled about why you want X.
- I'm curious about your reasons for proposing X.
- Explain to me how this solution might work for both of us.
- Well, that's an interesting idea. What other ideas do you have that might work for both of us?
- What do you think will happen if we don't find a creative solution that meets the needs and interests of both of us?
- What would you suggest I tell my team (group, organization, etc.) if we don't create a solution that meets everyone's needs and interests?
- What standards do you think we should use to resolve this issue?
- What might be an innovative idea that would allow us all to get what we want?

You may find, for example, that even though you've been locked in an epic battle with Barbara the Bitch in accounting about the way you do your reports, what she really wants is a more reasonable workload—something over which you have no control. Once you learn that this is the issue, however, you can at least commiserate, and conspire with her to win more resources for accounting during the next budget hassle.

Identifying the other person's underlying needs and interests when you're stuck in a recycled conflict, or when the person is trying to stonewall or win at all costs, requires that you engage in detective work. What's most important is that you listen and try to understand the other person's story.

When we're in conflict, we always have a story—a plot line, if you will—usually one that justifies our proposed solution.

If we focus on listening and ask open-ended questions as outlined in the previous list, eventually the other person or parties will reveal a clue that will lead us to their underlying need or interest—the real issue that they're withholding and not talking about. For pit bulls intent on winning at all costs, for example, we may discover they need a way to save face. They may need to take a time-out to consider their real options. You may be able to find a small point to give them an unimportant win that will help them save face.

All of this, of course, also requires that we identify our own needs and interests and avoid positions. This is the most important step in so-called interest-based conflict management and negotiation. The premise of this system is that it is possible for people to gain most or all of what the disputants want if they are willing to continue talking until they come up with a creative solution. This is the most powerful tool in your ability to unstick a recurring conflict.

THE POWER OF NEGOTIATION

Other kinds of negotiation systems focus on helping you win the most for your side. Those systems tend to focus on short-term gain for one party rather than long-term gains for both parties and for the relationship or the entire organization. In a workplace, you'd best assume that you will be there for the duration, and that therefore, creating a good working relationship remains an important goal. Although you can leave a job in which you can't creatively manage the conflict, this is an expensive (although popular) solution—both in terms of emotion and money.

In addition, even if you exit a job because of destructive conflict, you may meet your nemesis again. This is true in many industries; the world is becoming a very small place. You never know when you might run into Barbara the B---- again.

A need or interest is the underlying reason why we think we must have our way in any dispute. It is the reason why we think our solution is the best. In this form of conflict management, you must agree—to at least some extent—to be vulnerable, to reveal why you want something and to declare what's really important to you about an issue. Many people are afraid to do this, especially at work. We're fearful that if we acknowledge an underlying need or interest, the issue will be used against us.

Could this happen? Absolutely! I don't want to suggest that other people will always play fair or show sympathy. What I do know, however, is that it is difficult to formulate sustainable agreements if we are unwilling to reveal our underlying needs.

What happens instead is that if one party wins and the other feels cheated, the "loser" will exact revenge against the winner at some future point during the implementation of the agreement through foot dragging, sabotage, or other forms of passive-aggressive behavior. If we don't stop to understand the real needs of the parties, the solution we reach may not be the best or most creative for everyone over the long haul. In addition, we may not be considering the needs of the customers, clients, coworkers, or shareholders that the parties represent, which could lead to a fatal flaw in any suggested solution.

The other reason to reveal our own needs and interests is because people at work usually know how we feel even if we don't tell them. If you asked Barbara, for example, what she thinks her nickname might be in the office, I'll bet she could tell you!

Certainly, we don't need to reveal everything at work or in any negotiation; that's never smart. Yet, if we can be the first to open the door and be just a little bit vulnerable, we will witness miracles in our negotiations.

In contrast, if we stay stuck on arguing for our positions, the conflict may never be managed creatively. The classic story used to illustrate this difference is about two sisters and an orange. Two sisters lived in an isolated house, far from any convenience store. They had only one orange in the house and they both believed they needed and wanted the orange. If they stay stuck on their position of "I want the orange," the conflict is unlikely to be managed creatively.

They may decide to compromise—an idea that's considered enlightened by many in our society. If they compromise in this situation, they might decide to cut the orange in half. Compromise frequently results in a very interesting situation: both parties end up with half of what they thought they wanted!

In contrast, if the sisters are willing to reveal their underlying needs and interests, they may be able to find a creative way to meet all of them. For example, why might someone need an orange? They might need one for cooking, juggling, making a pomander, painting a still life of fruit, or for many other reasons.

In this situation, if one sister wants the juice of an orange to bake a cake and the other wants to use the peel (the zest of the orange) to bake a muffin, they are both able to receive what they want—if they're willing to be vulnerable enough to say why they want the orange.

Revealing our underlying needs frequently sparks creative solutions. If we're concealing our true interests, it's hard to fuel an innovative solution. In addition to being unwilling to be vulnerable, we may also fail to reveal our needs and interests because we fall in love with our solution; we become attached to our conclusion as the best or only way. Sometimes we even choose our friends based on our solutions. We favor only those who agree with us.

The following table shows some additional examples of positions, needs, and interests that may help you understand the difference.

POSITION	INTEREST
You must stop chewing gum!	I need quiet. You pop too loud!
I have to transfer.	I need Jill to stop micromanaging.
Stop telling me what to do!	I need you to appreciate what I do right.

These advanced conflict techniques can help unstick a repetitive conflict. First, though, we need to make sure the parties are paying attention in the first place.

Five Steps to Get Anyone to Listen to What You Have to Say

Sometimes it does need to be "all about us," but first we need to make sure that we approach someone in the right way. Needing to be right, recycling conflicts, fighting about surface issues instead of those underlying, and failing to reveal our own underlying need or interest are all ways that doom us to failure. What we need to do instead is to make sure that we try something (anything!) different to get this much-needed attention.

The truth is, most people these days have modern ADD; what psychiatrist and author Edward Hallowell calls "a severe case of modern life." Or what Linda Stone, the technologist who labeled the disease of the Internet age "continuous partial attention"—two people doing six things, devoting only partial attention to each one. As Stone points out, "We're so accessible, we're inaccessible. We can't find the off switch on our devices or on ourselves. . . . . We want to wear an iPod as much to listen to our own playlists as to block out the rest of the world and protect ourselves from all that noise. We are everywhere—except where we actually are physically." Thomas Friedman, the *New York Times* columnist, calls this the "age of interruption." He observes that he was much smarter when he could do only one thing at a time.

With all this noise, how do you catch someone's attention? Considering the inattentive age in which we live, here are five steps to make sure that people are actually listening to what you have to say:

1. Make sure that they (and you) turn off all cell phones, "crack berries," beeping watches, and small TVs on which they're watching the pregame show. In my seminars I always threaten to give any cell phones that beep, burp, or ring to my thirteen-year-old twins, who are dying for cell phones. "We'll see," I announce cheerfully, "how many minutes they can rack up in one week!" Use whatever means you have, whether it's humor, threats (short of violence), or rewards, just make sure that you have their undivided and unplugged attention.

2. Find out what they need to have in order to listen. An apology, a better time, or meeting at a coffee shop or bar instead of the office may all lead to more productive discussions. Find out what setting would be most comfortable for them. They may not have ever thought about what they need to have in order to listen but everyone has something.

3. Find out what motivates them. You can ask and ask and ask but if there's no motivation on their side, you

will not get the results you need and want. You may have to collect some intelligence to find out. Go ask Norma Know-It-All; every workplace has one. You know Norma. She's the person who always possesses more information than she should about everyone's promotions, office affairs, and facelifts. Your adversary may be motivated by understanding, help with a difficult project, a promise to fix her up with your brother, or your famous chocolate chip cookies.

4. Remind them of their promises. I hope that you've used the techniques in Chapter 6 to ask them to do what you want. If so, remind them of their promises and state something such as, "You've agreed to this but it's still not happening. What's in the way of this?" **Warning:** Do not ask this question in a snippy tone of voice (you know, the one that drove your mother nuts). Ask in a kind and sincere way. Feigned confusion works well in these encounters. Make statements such as, "I'm puzzled why this hasn't happened." "I'm confused by (whatever they did instead of what you asked.)"

5. Document the meeting and e-mail a summary of your discussion and agreement to them. Also send it to your (or their) supervisor if that person has been involved.

If You Must Escalate, Do It with Style

Once you've tried all these last-ditch conflict techniques, then, and only then, should you escalate. Sometimes, you do need to appeal to a higher authority: your manager, HR, the president of the company, or whomever. When you do, make sure that you've tried everything else first, and, most important, that you've documented all these attempts. After each conversation in which you try to resolve the problem, for example, send your combatant an e-mail confirming what you discussed and what he or she agreed to do. So that you don't sound like a nag, try to do it in a friendly, upbeat style such as this: "Just so I don't forget, here's what I think we agreed upon. I'm very spacy these days, so I like to write things down so that I remember." Remember, the one person in the room that it's always safe to make fun of is yourself.

When you document all incidents of bad behavior of your workplace nemeses, be specific, not conclusory. You want to document specific verifiable facts, not opinions, biases, or assumptions. How do you know that something is verifiable? I like to suggest that it has sensory detail: something you heard, saw, touched, or smelled. If it's something someone said, document that in quotes. It's a fact, for example, that Jerry came to you and said "Sue sexually harassed me too." It's not a fact if you write down "Sue sexually harassed Jerry," *unless* you observed that happening.

Without documentation, you really don't have much of a chance these days taking things to HR or your manager. Everyone is documenting, so HR expects a paper or e-mail trail. When I conduct workplace investigations these days, I'm always amazed at what employees are documenting. I sometimes wonder how they could possibly get any work done; all they're doing is documenting! I always advise managers that they need to document as well so that they win the war of documentation. They don't want to end up with the employees having better documentation than they do.

Here are some examples of the difference between conclusory and specific, verifying documentation:

CONCLUSORY	SPECIFIC/VERIFIABLE
Betsy's attitude sucks.	Betsy refused to talk to me yesterday.
Betsy's a witch.	Betsy threw a file at me when I asked for my reimbursement.
Betsy needs to adjust her medication.	Betsy was laughing hysterically and jumped up and down on her desk with no clothes on when I walked in on Friday.

Be sure to note the date and time the specific behavior occurred, and whether there was a witness.

Before you approach your higher authority, make sure that you review your organization's policies on complaints. You may be required to present your concerns to a specific person or in a specific format. Your policy should state that your complaints will be handled confidentially and that you'll be protected from retaliation. If your policy doesn't include this kind of protection, you may want to consult an attorney or your state's fair labor practices board or fair employment and housing board first.

When you do sit down with HR or your manager with your complaint, try to stay unemotional. Present the facts and make a specific doable request: something that person can do, not something that resides within someone else's authority. Don't ask, for example, for them to allow you to present your reimbursement requests to someone else if Betsy is the only employee in accounting. Don't ask to be transferred to another office if you know the CEO has frozen all transfer requests.

Try to convince your supervisor or HR to agree upon the follow-up or next steps. Ask when you can expect them to get back to you. Follow up with an e-mail thanking them for listening and telling them that you look forward to whatever resolution they've suggested.

It's not always easy to know what we need, and because of that, the exercise of documenting specific facts can sometimes challenge us. We're more adept at whining than really articulating our underlying needs. We need to break this cycle and talk about what we do want, not what we don't want. Also—and this can't be reiterated enough—you *must* have these conversations in person, not through e-mail. If the individual works in another location use the phone, but you at least need to wait to start talking until you have a live voice at the other end of the phone. Then follow up with an e-mail or letter summarizing your conversation in writing.

Consulting Outside Authorities

At some point in this process, you may want to consult an outside attorney, your union representative, your state's fair labor practices board, the Workers' Compensation Commission, or the Equal Employment Opportunity Commission. Even if you decide not to pursue a claim through these agencies, you may want to seek their advice first. Most of these agencies have publications and online resources that explain your specific rights in different situations. If you decide to consult a private attorney for advice, seek a referral from your state bar association. Attorneys are very specialized these days; you want someone who specializes in employee, not management, issues.

Be aware that you can seek an attorney's advice for a specific question in confidence, without your employer becoming aware that you've done so. When you call to set up an appointment, find out what the attorney's fee is for a specific amount of time and make sure that he or she has agreed to that before you begin the meeting.

Attorneys are bound to confidentiality. They can also advise you as you complain to and negotiate with your employer, without revealing that they're ever involved. Sort of like your own private wizard!

Before you talk with any of these outside authorities, you may want to do your own legal research on your rights and responsibilities. I've listed some reliable sources in the Resources section (Appendix A) of this book. If, for example, your workplace difficulties involve workers' compensation claims, wage and hour disputes, or discrimination, it helps to be educated before you complain. Knowledge is power in these situations.

If all of these efforts also fail, you may want to just walk on, which is the subject of the next chapter.

YOUR RELATIONSHIP TOOLBOX

HOW TO MOVE FROM PISSED OFF TO POWERFUL

PISSED OFF	POWERFUL
Throwing up your hands when a conflict recycles	Using last-ditch conflict techniques
Complaining or whining	Asking specifically for what you want
Documenting complaints that include biases or conclusions	Documenting verifiable facts
Complaining on e-mail	Talking in person

17.

WHEN YOU CAN'T "LOVE THE ONE YOU'RE WITH"

How to create a plan to move on.

Sally walked along the new outdoor mall, blind to the brilliant blue Colorado sky and deaf to the laughter of children playing in the outdoor fountain. Nothing could brighten her mood. She noticed the planter and the decorative retaining wall on the curb but didn't care to know if her architectural firm had designed them or not. At one point she'd taken great pride in the work her firm provided to the world. As one of the group's PR mavens, she had written books and articles trumpeting their success but now she could care less about their progress. Her new boss of the last six months—alternately overbearing, irritating, condescending, or sugary sweet—had drained her of any pleasure in her work. She'd read all the books, and tried everything they suggested, but nothing worked. She needed out NOW!

Throwing In the Towel

It is a useful exercise, as we've discussed in previous chapters, to learn how to "love the one you're with" but at some point, even the best of us need to fold our cards, pack up our tent, and move on. How do you know if it's your time? Take this test, answering yes or no for each item:

- You honestly do not have a bad habit of leaving jobs at the first sign of difficulty or conflict.
- You've diligently tried all the tricks in this book in order to improve your chances of loving your current job and managing the difficult people with whom you work.
- You're constantly miserable.
- Your mental or physical health is suffering because of your job.
- You're being subjected to mental or physical abuse or harassment.
- Your spouse, best friend, significant other, priest, and/or therapist is telling you that he or she can't stand to hear about your crummy work situation one more time.

If the answer is yes to two or more of these questions, you need, as U2 advises, to "Walk On."

Disaster Preparedness

Before you do make your move, however, be prepared. Consider these essential truths:

1. It is much easier to get a job when you have a job.
2. Burned bridges are difficult to rebuild.
3. An updated resume and a financial cushion should be in place, if possible, before you leave.
4. You may need emotional and financial support during the process.

Before, during, and after your move, one thing to be aware of is that you will most likely go through a process of grieving, even if you believe that the move is ultimately for the best. Because most of us are comforted by the familiar, we go through classic and predictable stages of leaving the old ways whenever we have to learn or do something new. Elisabeth Kübler-Ross, the famous therapist and death and dying expert, outlined this process. In her experience in working with many people who were dying, she learned that there are five stages to the process. Other theorists have realized that those stages are the predictable stages of *all loss*, not just death.

The first stage is *denial*. You deny that the loss is necessary or even happening. You want to avoid the move, change, or loss, and ignore all of the warning signs.

The next stage is *anger*. At this stage you realize that the change is inevitable and start railing at the universe in anger about the fact that it's occurring. You may lash out at those closest to you, or your anger may turn inward and you may find yoursef dealing with depression. It's common at this stage to be unaware of the real source of your anger.

The third stage is *bargaining*: trying to negotiate with whatever power or gods you believe in, promising that you'll do or say anything if the change doesn't happen. Like desperate gamblers, you may promise piety or your firstborn child in order to avoid the loss.

The fourth stage is *depression*. You realize that bargaining won't work and you feel a deep sadness, usually disguised as depression, over this realization.

Acceptance is when you realize that the gig is up: this terrible thing really is going to happen. You accept that the change will occur, adjust your life accordingly, and plan for the future.

The application of this system in the workplace is important. You need to work your way through all five stages before you can really be present and available to your soul to discover what you want to do next. *It is critical that you not make a final decision about what to do next until you've worked your way through all the stages, unless your emotional and/or physical health makes that impossible.*

Be aware that most people do not travel through these stages on a straight line. You may proceed with one step forward, two steps backward. Yet if you're aware of the grief process and if you chart your progress, you generally move in an upward spiral to resolution and acceptance.

When you're faced with the possibility of a new idea or change, you must take stock of where you are in the grieving process and work though your feelings. The only way around these feelings is through them. If you deny they exist, you block the energy that you could use more successfully for the future. If you sink too deeply into any stage, especially depression, you can become mired in analysis paralysis and fail to move.

It is easy to get stuck at any stage of the process. Anger (gone inward as depression) is certainly the most common, but it can happen at any of the other stages also. Many people, in fact, can stay stuck in anger and its twin, depression, for most of their lives, unable to move on after being blindsided by a big loss. In order to avoid this fate, you need to make sure that you work your way through all of the stages of loss. You may need the help of a mental health professional, minister, or priest in order to do so. Grief work truly is work.

Various kinds of expressive endeavors, such as art, dance, and music, can also be helpful in moving you along the path. The trick is to do something—not just sit back passively and assume that your emotions will take care of themselves. Taking care of your emotions responsibly, through one of these methods, is just as essential as taking care of your body through diet, exercise, and visits to a health-care practitioner.

The other paradigm that I've found useful in moving through these stages is that of William Bridges, PhD, whose classic book *Transitions: Making Sense of Life's Changes* also provides help for the journey through the maze of walking on. In his system, it's not the new idea that most people are avoiding; it's the sometimes painful, disruptive, and scary movement through the transition. His theory is that transition involves three distinct phases and that failure to complete any particular phase can lead to an incomplete and unnecessarily painful transition.

The three Bridges phases are:

Endings. The old has ended but the new has not begun. In order to move on, you need to acknowledge the old. This is the phase at which many difficulties appear. Bridges recommends that people consciously plan "funerals" or other rituals that commemorate this phase.

The Neutral Zone. The old has ended but the new way is not clear. I call this the chaos zone, because "the neutral zone" sounds much too benign to me. Many chaotic events occur in this zone, and it's easy to become lost and confused. Bridges uses the analogy of Moses leading people through the desert for forty years, during which time people must have been totally frustrated and questioning how Moses could possibly know what he was doing! Can you imagine being Moses? Every day he had to get up and convince people. "All right! Another great day of marching! Only twenty more years left!"

The New Beginning. At this point the new way is clear. Bridges recommends that people also celebrate this phase by marking it with some ceremonial or ritual gesture.

All of these issues occur in groups. For example, one of my clients began a large-scale reorganization effort designed to change the company's command-and-control environment to a more inclusive one. The CEO expected employees to love the changes, because they would have more input into decision-making. Much to his surprise, however, workers balked. They questioned the changes, carped that the proposal was too complex, and generally stalled on implementing new processes and procedures.

At first the executive team assumed that the employees were resisting the change itself, so they charged ahead with a series of focus groups to better inform people about why they were installing the new methods and procedures. What the groups revealed, however, was that workers didn't object to the goal. What they were resisting was the transition process. Their number one question was, "What resources are going to be available to help me do my job during this transition?" Without knowing *how* they personally could get through the change, the workers wanted no part in understanding the *why* behind the change.

What tools and resources do you need to get you through your particular change? Consider the following list: psychological help, career coaching, or spiritual support; more information about your legal rights; or perhaps Friday night out with the girls, drinking margaritas.

Please take all the time you need to determine what support you need to get through this transition. Certainly friends and relatives can be helpful (although you should stay away from those nervous nellies who question your need to leave a "perfectly good job"), but you may also need to seek professional support from a job counselor, therapist, minister, or other counselor. Such professionals can provide the objectivity that others lack. If you're the graduate of a college or university, your alma mater may allow you to come back and use its career support services long after you've graduated.

Yes, Virginia, There Is a Santa Claus

Sometimes when you leave a job, you may be able to do so with your pockets full of money (or at least a check). At a minimum, you want to research using all your sick leave and vacation time. Also, be sure to find out whether your health insurance can stay intact if you're going to be unemployed for a while. A federal law called COBRA (Consolidated Omnibus Budget Reconciliation Act) requires your employers to offer you the option of keeping your insurance for some period of time. You might want to explore any other legal rights you might have.

GET THE LAW ON YOUR SIDE

A one-time consultation with an attorney can pay off. Employment law, as with most other areas of the law, is quite specialized these days. Because employment lawyers specialize in representing plaintiffs (employees) or defendants (employers), you need to be sure to find someone who specializes in plaintiff's employment law, preferably as all or most of his or her practice. Ask your local bar association or the National Employment Lawyers Association (NELA) for a referral.

What legal claims might you have? Sally, for example, the depressed PR person for the architectural firm, walked on when her boss tried to change her long-standing schedule. Because of health problems, she'd always worked four short days. Her new boss basically took a take-it-or-leave-it attitude. "This is the job you have," she sniffed.

Sally consulted an attorney who analyzed her situation under the Family and Medical Leave Act (FMLA), which provides that employees have the right to take off up to twelve weeks a year (unpaid) to take care of their own health situation or the health problems of their immediate family members. You're not required to take all twelve weeks at the same time, as long as you can document the need to take the days at different times. The attorney also looked at whether Sally had any partial disability claims. Though the attorney was unable to determine for sure whether Sally had any claims, she helped Sally draft a letter outlining her concerns and advised her what to request from her employer.

In a panic, Sally called her attorney in the middle of the negotiations. "I'm afraid that they'll think I've talked to an attorney if I say what you've suggested," she whined.

"So?" responded Ms. Attorney.

"But then it will turn into a confrontation."

"So?" repeated Ms. Attorney.

"But then they might get upset at me!"

"So?"

You get the picture. Taking this tack may require nerves of steel and some outside coaching, but Sally walked away with a severance package that allowed her four months to determine what she wanted to do next.

I'm not advising that you should make something up; however, if your employer hasn't respected your legal rights, you may want to explore your options. What other legal claims might you have? Discrimination or harassment, of course. Be aware, however, that generic bad behavior is not discrimination or harassment. You need to prove that your boss or coworkers treated you badly because of your age, race, sex, disability, sexual orientation, and so on. There is an overview of many of these legal claims in Chapter 3.

You may also have a claim for *constructive discharge*. This term describes the outcome of a situation in which a boss wants to get rid of an employee but is afraid to fire him or her, so the boss starts treating the employee badly by changing the work schedule or assigning undesirable work and difficult or impossible-to-reach deadlines. The employee then gives up and quits. Instead of suing for wrongful termination, the employee sues for constructive discharge, which means that your situation at work has become so intolerable that a reasonable person would quit.

Many times these kinds of claims do not involve an actual lawsuit—a potentially career-ending move in some industries in which everyone knows everyone else. Instead, an attorney can simply advise you of your rights, and you do the negotiation on your own. Alternatively, an attorney may negotiate an out-of-court settlement for you before any lawsuit is ever filed.

If you think that anything like what's been described here may be happening to you, it is well worth your while to spend the money for a one-time visit to an attorney. Find out ahead of time exactly what you will be charged for this visit. You might also want to call the local bar association or any law schools in your area to determine whether there are any free or reduced-fee clinics available to you.

You Can Come Home Again, If You're Smart

The famously successful consulting firm McKinsey & Company got where it is by doing things the smart way, sometimes taking untraditional steps. One of those has been to encourage what it calls "boomerangs," people who leave the firm but may come back. Boomerangs have their own McKinsey-sponsored parties, newsletters, reunions, and blogs. These people are smart enough to know that it's a small world, and the McKinsey name and goodwill means something to them. The firm's smart enough to realize that there may come a time when it makes sense for them to welcome back a former employee with open arms.

Don't burn bridges—they're hard to rebuild once you do. I realize that this may seem contrary to the advice in the previous section about seeking legal counsel, but if you don't have a need to push your legal claim, or don't need one, don't take it. The goodwill and possibility of returning may be worth much more to you than whatever the settlement may be.

When I left my 17th Street (Denver's Wall Street) firm, I was the only woman partner. Although I had my gripes and quibbles, I basically liked the firm. I just knew that I was, at heart, a teacher and that I wanted to write and teach.

Before I made a public announcement I met with the key players privately to let them know what I was doing, how much I'd learned from working with each of them, and how much I had appreciated their support. I made sure that they understood that it was what I wanted and needed to do and that it had nothing to do with the firm or its treatment of me. I knew that they—and the Street—were sensitive to claims that the firm couldn't keep women.

Although there was some complaining—and I know that some of them thought I was nuts to leave the security, prestige, and money of the firm—they accepted my resignation gracefully. Since I left, the firm has asked me to do some consulting and training for them, and I've also been a client of the firm. You never know on what planet you may ultimately land.

Leave Them Wanting More

No matter how tempting it may be to "check out" once you know you're leaving, do not leave projects unfinished. Do what your mother told you to do—clean up any messes that you made before you leave. Do not write Good Riddance letters to the tyrants and boors you worked with on your way out the door. Do not go on the company blog and trash your old employer. Be gracious. Be charming if it kills you. The world is becoming a very small place.

Search for Your Next Gig with Grace and Integrity

One of the problems these days is finding a new job when your former employer won't give you a reference. Like many people, employers are lawsuit paranoid. They're afraid of being sued for defamation (saying something false about someone) or discrimination (saying something good about one person but not another), so they just refuse to do anything. You do have a smart solution to this pickle, however. You can ask for and copy all of your performance reviews. Assuming they're good, you can take them with you. They will speak even louder than a reference.

Although the Web is a great job-finding resource, and I've listed some suggested sites in the Resources section (Appendix A) of this book, most people still find jobs the old-fashioned way: through personal contact.

Be bold. Tell everyone from your mother-in-law to your mailman what you're looking for. Follow up on all leads. Treat the search as a job in itself. Since looking can be discouraging, having a job counselor or employment support group can be helpful. Find the support you need.

Some additional tips:
Don't panic. Use whatever stress relief techniques you can find to keep your cool. When you move out of a bad

STOP Pissing Me Off!

situation, it builds character. Realize that you made a mistake, be honest about your error, and know that fixing it is something new employers will appreciate.

Experiment with new careers. Internships and temporary assignments aren't just for students anymore. If you're considering a new field or industry, find a short-term contract position or volunteer to work free. You'll get a firsthand look at the workload, culture, and potential, something no interview will give you.

Know your quarry. With the Internet, there's no excuse for not researching a potential employer before you write or meet with them. Be sure to mention what you've learned in your cover letter or job interview. Find out as much as possible.

Project positive energy. A dynamite resume will get you in the door, but employers really decide based upon the personal characteristics that they believe can get the job done, that elusive thing called chemistry. Shine on. Don't be too cool to show your energy and enthusiasm, and save the trashing of your current (or former) employer for your spouse or therapist. Just mention that it wasn't the right fit for you, and change the subject.

The Light at the End of the Tunnel

Singer Josh Groban tells the story of how his life changed between seventh and eighth grades. As the boy who liked to sing his own songs at talent shows, he became "suddenly uncool." His school loved athletes and star students; Groban was neither. At the end of his eighth-grade year a friend gave him a brochure for the Los Angeles County High School for the Arts—an audition-based public school where you study academics for the first half of the day and dedicate the second half to your chosen art. He auditioned and was accepted. Forced to perform a monologue on the first day of class, he was sure he'd made another mistake. He was amazed to find that as he tried to slink away after class, one person complimented him; another asked him to join him for lunch. Behind him, he noticed two people reciting lines from a play and beyond that someone singing opera. Groban had found "the only high school in the world where I even had a chance of being cool."

Since then, he's had much pressure to conform or go against his heart, but instead of doing either, he remembers this experience. He had to walk on and away from an unsupportive environment, however, in order to find his true place.

As you may have guessed from reading this book, I'm one of those unusual people who actually likes working. I started my first paying job (other than chores on the ranch where I grew up) at sixteen as a lifeguard at a public swimming pool, where we not only guarded little children splashing us from the pool but also cleaned the restrooms, taught swim lessons, and sold snacks. I loved my job! (Well, cleaning restrooms, not so much, but the rest of it . . .) After that I worked my way through college and law school as a waitress, a secretary, dishwasher, and dorm room counselor. As an attorney I've worked in government agencies, private law firms, as a law school professor, and as a contract attorney, associate, and partner. Now I have my own business, which includes writing books, speaking, and consulting. Although I liked all my other work, I felt that when I started my own business, I'd finally reached the place where I could breathe, just as Groban did at the High School for the Arts.

I have no doubt that you can find your own place and that, indeed, everyone has one.I truly believe that we all came to earth with gifts, things that we need to exercise in order to be truly happy and successful. You matter. What you do matters, no matter what job you're in. If you keep experimenting until you find the thing that you love to do and then do that work with intensity and focus, success and fulfillment are sure to follow.

My thoughts and prayers go with you as you walk on.

YOUR RELATIONSHIP TOOLBOX

HOW TO MOVE FROM PISSED OFF TO POWERFUL

PISSED OFF	POWERFUL
Staying in a job where you're miserable	Leaving once you've tried every other possible solution
Failing to go through the grieving process	Doing the grief work
Leaving impulsively	Planning a graceful exit
Trashing people on your way out	Being charming even if it kills you
Going it alone	Getting all the support you need
Leaving money on the table	Consulting an attorney

CONCLUSION

Life is difficult, as M. Scott Peck reminds us in *The Road Less Traveled,* but once we accept that fact, life becomes easier. It's all a matter of adjusting our expectations.

Working with difficult people presents the same contradiction: If you expect everyone to be easy to work with, your working life will be difficult; if you adjust your expectations, the path smoothes out.

Working with difficult people is an essential workplace skill, well worth your time to learn and hone, just as you would learn to play the piano or program a computer. Without this skill, your working life may well be miserable.

The reality is that difficult people work everywhere. I hope this book has helped you see that difficult people are not the enemy; they're just yet another blip on the radar screen of your day. An annoyance, perhaps, but one that you have the tools to overcome, not something that needs to wreck your day or your basic career satisfaction.

Doing work you love is one of life's great pleasures. Don't stop searching until you find out what that is. And remember to stop and have fun as you journey through various workplace experiments.

Go out there. Be well. Be wise. Work well and don't let the difficult people steal from you the joys and pleasures of a successful career. I wish you the best on your journey.

May the force be with you.

APPENDIX A
ADDITIONAL RESOURCES

9to5, National Association of Working Women
www.9to5.org

American Civil Liberties Union
www.aclu.org

American Federation of Labor–Congress of Industrial Organizations (AFL-CIO)
www.aflcio.org

American Psychological Association
www.apa.org

Asian American Legal Defense and Educational Fund (AALDEF)
E-mail: *AALDEF@worldnet.att.net*

Equal Employment Opportunity Commission (EEOC)
www.eeoc.gov

American Academy of Family Physicians
www.familydoctor.org

Good Clean Funnies List
www.gcfl.net

Laughter Yoga
www.laughteryoga.org

Lynne Eisaguirre, Workplaces That Work

www.workplacesthatwork.com

Mexican American Legal Defense and Educational Fund (MALDEF)
www.maldef.org

Micro Expression Training Tool (METT) CD available at
www.PaulEkman.com

Mind and Life Institute
www.mindandlife.org

NAACP Legal Defense and Education Fund, Inc.
www.naacp.org

National Employment Lawyers Association (NELA)
www.nela.org

National Institute of Mental Health (NIMH)
www.nimh.nih.gov

National Organization for Women (NOW)
www.now.org

Legal Momentum
(formerly Now Legal Defense and Education Fund)
www.legalmomentum.org

The National Sleep Foundation
www.sleepfoundation.org

Thorax: An International Journal of Respiratory Medicine
www.thorax.bmj.com

Working America

www.workingamerica.org/badboss

APPENDIX B
BIBLIOGRAPHY

Bokur, Debra. "What's So Funny?" *Yoga Journal*, February, 2007.

Britten, Rhonda. *Fearless Living*. New York: Perigee Trade (reprint edition), 2002.

Bridges, William. *Transitions: Making Sense of Life's Changes*. Reading, MA: Addison-Wesley, 1980.

Buckingham, Marcus. *Go Put Your Strengths to Work: 6 Powerful Steps to Achieve Outstanding Performance*. New York: Free Press, 2007.

Burns, David D. *Feeling Good: The New Mood Therapy*, revised and updated. New York: Avon, 1999.

Charan, Ram. "Why CEOs Fail." *Fortune*, June 21, 1999, p. 69.

Csikszentmihalyi, Mihaly. *Flow: The Psychology of Optimal Experience*. New York: Harper Perennial (reprint edition), 1991.

Eisaguirre, Lynne. *The Power of a Good Fight*. Indianapolis: Literary Architects, 2006.

Fiorina, Carly. *Tough Choices: A Memoir*. New York: Portfolio, 2006.

Forni, P. M. *Choosing Civility: The Twenty-Five Rules of Considerate Conduct*. New York: St. Martin's/Griffin (reprint edition), 2003.

Frankl, Viktor E. *Man's Search for Meaning*, revised and updated. Boston: Beacon Press, 1996.

Goldberg, Natalie. *The Great Failure: A Bartender, a Monk, and My Unlikely Path to Truth*. San Francisco: HarperCollins, 2004.

Gilbert, Daniel. *Stumbling on Happiness*. New York: Knopf, 2006.

Goleman, Daniel. *Emotional Intelligence: Why It Can Matter More Than IQ.* New York: Bantam (reprint edition), 1997.

———. *Social Intelligence: The New Science of Human Relationships.* New York: Bantam, 2006.

Hallowell, Edward M. *Connect.* New York: Pantheon, 1999.

Hendricks, Gay. *Conscious Living: Finding Joy In the Real World.* San Francisco: Harper San Francisco, 2001.

Jamison, Kathy Redfield. *An Unquiet Mind.* New York: Picador (new edition), 1997.

Peck, M. Scott. *The Road Less Traveled.* New York: Simon & Schuster, 1978.

Porter, Gayle. "Workaholics as High-Performance Employees: The Intersection of Workplace and Family Relationship Problems." In *High-Performance Families: Causes, Consequences, and Clinical Solutions,* ed. B. Robinson and N. Chase, a monograph in the American Counseling Association's Family Psychology and Counseling Series, pp. 43–69. Alexandria, VA: American Counseling Association, 2001.

Preston, Stephanie D. and Frans B. M. de Waal. "Empathy: Its Ultimate and Proximate Bases." *Behavioral and Brain Sciences* 25 (2002), pp. 1–20.

Robinson, Bryan E. *Chained to the Desk: A Guidebook for Workaholics, Their Partners and Children, and the Clinicians Who Treat Them.* New York: New York University Press, 2001.

Schor, Juliet B. *The Overworked American: The Unexpected Decline of Leisure.* New York: Basic Books, 1991.

Seligman, Martin. *Authentic Happiness.* Boston: Nicholas Brealey Publishing, Ltd., 2003.

———. *Learned Optimism: How to Change Your Mind and Your Life.* New York: Vintage (reprint), 2006.

Slater, Robert. *29 Leadership Secrets from Jack Welch,* 2nd ed. New York: McGraw-Hill, 2003.

Somer, Elizabeth, and Nancy Snyderman. *Food & Mood: The Complete Guide to Eating Well and Feeling Your Best,* 2nd ed. New York: Owl Books, 1999.

Stern, Daniel. *The Present Moment in Psychotherapy and Everyday Life*. New York: W. W. Norton, 2004.

Suskind, Ron. *The One Percent Doctrine: Deep Inside America's Pursuit of Its Enemies Since 9/11*. New York: Simon & Schuster, 2006.

Sutherland, Amy. *Kicked, Bitten, and Scratched: Life and Lessons at the World's Premier School for Exotic Animal Trainers*. New York: Viking, 2006.

Swenson, Richard, MD. *The Overload Syndrome: Learning to Live Within Your Limits*. Colorado Springs: NavPress Publishing Group, 1998.

Tannen, Deborah. *You Just Don't Understand: Women and Men in Conversation*. New York: William Morrow, 1990.

Ury, William. *Getting to Peace: Transforming Conflict at Home, at Work, and in the World*. New York: Viking, 1999.

Williams, Redford, MD, and Williams, Virginia, PhD. *In Control: No More Snapping at Your Family, Sulking at Work, Steaming in the Grocery Line, Seething at Meetings, Stuffing Your Frustration*. Emmaus, PA: Rodale Books, 2006.

INDEX